Gluten Free Mediterranean

By Sanaa

Publisher's Cataloging-in-Publication
(Provided by Quality Books, Inc.)

Abourezk, Sanaa.
Gluten free Mediterranean / by Sanaa.
p. cm.
Includes index.
ISBN-13: 978-0-9666627-1-9
ISBN-10: 0-9666627-1-7
1. Cookery, Mediterranean.
2. Gluten-free diet--Recipes. I. Title.
TX725.M35A26 2008 641.59'1822
QBI08-600241

Published by
Palmyra Publishing Company
401 E. 8th Street, Suite 321
Sioux Falls, SD 57103

To

Alya, my wonderful daughter,
who is the cure for any and all my ailments.

This book is dedicated to all of my customers,
especially those who have inspired the idea for this book,
and those who have been willing to become test subjects
by trying out my recipes and giving me
their honest opinion.

Introduction

For whatever reason, I am sensing that celiac disease, or the allergy to gluten, is on the increase. It may be that we are just hearing about it much more than we used to, or perhaps people are finding a diagnosis earlier, and the medical profession is more easily able to identify the disease.

Whatever the reason, the seriousness of the disease requires a serious attack on its causes, and how we can avoid its effects. I am hopeful that the medical research community will soon be able to find a cure, or, at least, some kind of relief of the symptoms caused by ingesting gluten. In the meantime, it is necessary for us to be able to live with it by avoiding the symptoms caused by gluten sensitivity.

As most gluten sensitive people know, gluten is a component of grains such as wheat, barley, rye, oats and their byproducts. These foods are easy to avoid as they are straightforward. But what is tricky for gluten sensitive people are the hidden grains in foods that we least suspect. It is critical that those who are gluten sensitive be always vigilant by carefully reading labels on the food packages they purchase. One cannot relax, thinking that a product they have purchased in the past is safe and gluten free. The reason for that is that food manufacturers have no qualms about changing the ingredients in their products. They will, unthinkingly, add a substance containing gluten that is dangerous for those with celiac disease. For example, manufacturers will add a stabilizer or a new flavoring or a food coloring that contains gluten. I don't accuse them of doing so deliberately, but they do it without thinking about the millions of Americans who cannot tolerate gluten in their food.

Gluten sensitive people find it necessary to educate themselves about terminology used by manufacturers on their labels. Even some toothpastes contain gluten, as well as seemingly innocent products as some children's play dough.

Some labels do not spell out the fact that the ingredients contain gluten, but if you get to know the terminology used by manufacturers, you can avoid damage to your system. Here are some ingredients that may contain gluten, without warning:

Starch
Hydrolized wheat gluten
Semolina
Anti-caking ingredients
Modified food starch
Emulsifiers
Flavoring
Monosodium glutamate.
Modified food starch.
Some soy sauces, depending on how it is made.
Malt vinegar
Some beers, most of which are made with barley
Bottled salad dressing

Table of Contents

Appetizers

Soups

Salads

Main Dishes

Baking and Desserts

APPETIZERS

Red Bell Pepper Spread

Serves 4-6

2 red bell peppers, seeded and cut into small pieces
1 medium onion, chopped
2 cups walnuts
3 tablespoons olive oil
1 tablespoon Harrisa*
2 tablespoons Pomegranate molasses*
1 teaspoon freshly ground cumin
2 teaspoons freshly ground coriander
salt to taste

• In a food processor, process all ingredients into a smooth paste.

Eggplant Caviar

Serves 4-6

3 1-pound eggplants
3 cloves garlic, mashed
3 tablespoons olive oil
3 tablespoons lemon juice
½ cup parsley, finely chopped
salt to taste

- With a fork, punch a couple of holes in each eggplant. Broil or grill the eggplant until the skin is charred.
- Cool and then peel the skin. Mash the eggplant into a smooth paste.
- Add the rest of the ingredients. Refrigerate for a couple of hours before serving.

Baba Ghanouj

Serves 4-6

3 1-pound eggplants
3 cloves garlic, mashed
3 cups plain yogurt
3 tablespoons Tahini*
salt to taste

- With a fork, punch a couple of holes in the eggplant. Broil or grill the eggplant until the skin is charred. Cool, peel the skin and mash the meat.
- Mix in the rest of the ingredients. Refrigerate for a couple of hours before serving.

Eggplant and Pepper Rolls

Makes 5 rolls

- 1 2-pound eggplant
- 1 red bell pepper
- ½ cup goat cheese
- 1 teaspoon thyme, chopped
- ¼ teaspoon cayenne pepper

- Peel the skin of the eggplant, and then cut lengthwise into ½-inch thick slices. Spray each slice with olive oil spray and broil on each side until golden.
- Roast the bell pepper until charred. Peel the skin and cut the pepper lengthwise into pieces.
- Mix the goat cheese with the thyme and the cayenne pepper.
- Lay out one slice of the eggplant, top with one bell pepper slice, and then place one teaspoon of the goat cheese mixture in the center. Roll into a 1-inch thick roll. Serve at room temperature.

Eggplant with Scallions and Yogurt

Serves 4-6

1 2-pound eggplant
3 scallions, chopped
1 clove garlic
2 cups plain yogurt
½ cup fresh cilantro, chopped
1 tablespoon olive oil
1 tablespoon lemon juice
salt and pepper to taste

- Place the peeled garlic clove inside the yogurt and refrigerate.
- Wash and cut the eggplant into half-inch thick slices. Place the eggplant slices on a cookie sheet, spray with olive oil spray and broil until golden. Turn over to the other side, spray and broil. Remove from the oven and allow to cool.
- Dice the eggplant and mix with the cilantro and the scallions.
- Whisk lemon juice with olive oil, salt and pepper. Drizzle over the eggplant mixture.
- Spoon the eggplant salad into a shallow serving platter.
- Remove the garlic from the yogurt, and then spoon the yogurt on top of the eggplant salad. Serve at room temperature.

Eggplant with Egg and Garlic Spread

Serves 4

2 1-pound eggplants
3 cloves garlic
4 tablespoons olive oil
2 eggs
salt and pepper to taste

- Make several thin cuts into each eggplant. Place in the oven and broil until charred or grill until charred. Remove from the heat and allow it to cool. Remove the skin and mash the pulp.
- Mix the mashed eggplants with the garlic, the salt and pepper.
- In a shallow frying pan, heat the olive oil and cook the eggs as though you are making scrambled eggs. Add the eggplant mixture to the eggs and continue to cook for a couple of minutes, stirring often, then serve.

Eggplant Spread with Sweet Pepper

Serves 4-6

2 1-pound eggplants
½ cup green bell pepper, finely chopped
½ cup red bell pepper, finely chopped
1 cup pomegranate seeds, optional
2 cloves garlic, mashed
2 tablespoons lemon juice
4 tablespoons olive oil

- Grill or broil the eggplants as in the previous recipe.
- Peel the skin and mash the pulp.
- Mix the pulp with the peppers, the pomegranate seeds, the mashed garlic, lemon juice and salt.
- Place the mixture in a shallow serving bowl, drizzle with olive oil and serve.

Ratatouille

Serves 4

1 medium onion, finely chopped
4 tablespoons olive oil
2 bell peppers, seeded and coarsely chopped
1 medium zucchini, cut into 2-inch thick cubes
1 clove garlic, mashed
2 tomatoes, finely diced
salt and pepper to taste

- Heat the olive oil in a heavy pan and sauté the onions for 5 minutes.
- Add the garlic, the peppers and the zucchini. Stir, cover and cook for 10 minutes.
- Add the tomatoes, the seasoning and stir gently. Cover and cook for 5 minutes.

Mango and Black Bean Dip

Serves 8

2 cups boiled black beans
¼ cup olive oil
1 medium onion, finely chopped
1 large red bell pepper, finely chopped
½ cup cilantro, chopped
1 large ripe mango, peeled, chop the flesh
½ teaspoon ground cumin
½ teaspoon ground coriander
salt and pepper to taste

- In a heavy skillet, heat olive oil and sauté the onion until translucent.
- Add the red bell pepper and the cilantro, stir and cook over medium heat for a couple of minutes.
- Add the rest of the ingredients, stir, cover and simmer for 5 minutes.
- Remove from the heat, adjust the seasoning and puree. Serve warm with corn chips.

Zucchini in Tahini Sauce

Serves 4

6 medium zucchinis
1 medium onion, chopped
½ cup Tahini*
½ cup lemon juice
2 cloves garlic, mashed
½ cup parsley, chopped
salt to taste

- Slice the zucchinis into half-inch thick rounds. Place the zucchinis on a cookie sheet, spray with olive oil and broil until golden. Remove from the oven and place in a baking dish.
- Sprinkle the zucchini with the chopped onions.
- Whisk the Tahini with the lemon juice, garlic and salt. If the sauce is thick, add little water and whisk into a smooth sauce. Drizzle the Tahini sauce over the onions.
- Cover with aluminum foil and bake in a 350 degree oven for 15 minutes.
- Remove from the oven. Remove the foil, sprinkle with the parsley and serve hot.

Rosemary Potato Rounds

Serves 4-6

1 large potato
2 tablespoons olive oil
1 clove garlic, mashed
1 tablespoon lemon juice
1 teaspoon fresh rosemary, chopped
1 tablespoon sour cream
1 teaspoon Parmesan cheese
salt to taste

- Cut each potato into 1-inch thick slices.
- Mix olive oil with lemon juice, garlic, rosemary and salt. Rub each potato slice with the rosemary mix.
- Place the potato slices on a cookie sheet, and then bake in a 375 degree oven for 40 minutes or until golden. Remove the potatoes from the oven, sprinkle with the Parmesan cheese and spoon a little sour cream on each slice. Serve hot.

Mushrooms with Cilantro

Serves 4

1 pound white mushrooms, sliced
¼ cup olive oil
1 clove garlic, mashed
1 cup fresh cilantro, chopped
1 tablespoon lemon juice
½ teaspoon coriander
½ teaspoon chili pepper
salt and pepper to taste

- In a skillet, heat the olive oil and sauté the mushroom slices until soft and golden.
- Add the garlic, the cilantro and the rest of the seasoning. Stir and cook over medium heat for a couple of minutes.
- Drizzle with lemon juice and serve hot.

Potato with Coriander

Serves 4

1 medium potato, peeled and cut into 1-inch cubes
1 tablespoon olive oil
1 medium onion, finely chopped
1 teaspoon ground coriander
salt and pepper to taste

- Bring salted water to a boil. Drop in the potatoes and allow the water to come back to a boil. Allow the potatoes to boil for a couple of minutes. Drain.
- In a heavy skillet, heat the olive oil and cook the onions until golden.
- Add the potatoes, stir and cook over medium heat for 5 minutes. Add the coriander, the salt and the pepper. Stir and cook for a couple of minutes.

Yogurt Cheese and Walnut Spread

Makes 2 cups

4 cups plain non-fat yogurt
½ cup walnuts, finely chopped and toasted
½ teaspoon dry mint
salt to taste

- Stir the yogurt, then spoon into cheesecloth. Allow the yogurt to drain overnight. What will remain is yogurt cheese that has the consistency of commercial cream cheese.
- Remove yogurt paste from the cheesecloth, add the rest of the ingredients and mix well.

Mint Yogurt Cheese

Makes 2 cups

- 4 cups plain yogurt
- 1 tablespoon dry mint
- ¼ teaspoon cayenne powder
- ½ teaspoon salt
- 2 teaspoons sesame seeds, toasted

- Stir the yogurt and the salt. Line a colander with two layers of cheesecloth, then pour the yogurt into cheesecloth.
- Place the colander over the sink and allow yogurt to drain for at least 6 hours.
- Remove the cheese from the colander, scoop the yogurt cheese into a container, and mix in the rest of the ingredients. Pack it firmly.

Cheese Thyme Balls

Makes 10 balls

6 cups plain yogurt
½ teaspoon salt
1 teaspoon black sesame seeds
1 teaspoon sesame seeds
2 teaspoons dry thyme
4 tablespoons olive oil

- Mix yogurt with salt. Line a colander with two layers of cheesecloth, then pour the yogurt into the cheesecloth. Place the colander over the sink and allow the yogurt to drain for 6 hours. Remove the yogurt cheese from the colander and place in a bowl.
- In a small bowl, mix black sesame seeds, sesame seeds and thyme.
- Scoop one tablespoon full of the yogurt cream cheese onto wax paper.
- Lightly moisten your palms with water. Roll the cream cheese into balls and then roll them in the thyme sesame mixture.
- Place in a flat serving dish, drizzle with the olive oil and serve.
- The cheese balls can be stored in a jar filled with olive oil.

Lettuce Rolls

Makes 12 rolls

12 tender Boston lettuce leaves
1 cup ricotta cheese
½ cup ground almonds, toasted
1 small cucumber, peeled, seeded and finely diced
1 teaspoon fresh tarragon, chopped
dash chili powder

- Drain and mash the cheese, and then mix with the rest of the ingredients, except for the lettuce leaves.
- Place a teaspoon of the cheese mixture on each lettuce leaf. Fold the leaf over the cheese and roll.

Roasted Peppers with Kalamata Olives

Serves 4-6

2 red bell peppers
2 yellow bell peppers
2 tablespoons olive oil
1 cup Kalamata olives, pitted and finely chopped
½ cup scallions, chopped
1 teaspoon oregano
1 tablespoon lemon juice
salt to taste

- Broil the pepper, cool and peel the skin. Remove the seeds, cut into thin slices and place in a shallow serving platter.
- Mix the olive oil with the lemon juice and the oregano.
- Sprinkle the chopped olives and scallions over the peppers, then drizzle the flavored olive oil over the peppers.

Artichoke Hearts with Herbs

Serves 4

4 artichokes
1 lemon, sliced
2 cloves garlic, sliced
1 red bell pepper, finely chopped
1 yellow bell pepper, finely chopped
2 scallions, finely chopped
1 cup parsley, chopped
2 tablespoons olive oil
¼ cup lemon juice
salt to taste

- Stem the artichokes close to the base. Scoop out the heart and trim the base to form a cup. In a heavy pot, bring eight cups of water to a boil. Drop the lemon slices, the garlic and the artichoke bottoms into the boiling water and cook until tender. Drain, and then set aside.
- Mix the rest of the ingredients and toss well.
- Place the artichoke bottoms on a shallow plate and spoon a little of the pepper mixture into each bottom.

Swiss Chard with Tahini Sauce

Serves 4

1 pound Swiss chard
3 tablespoons Tahini*
¼ cup lemon juice
2 tablespoons Pomegranate Molasses*
¼ cup water
4 cloves garlic, mashed
1 teaspoon ground cumin
salt to taste

- Cut the Swiss chard into small pieces. In a large pot, bring water to a boil. Drop the chopped Swiss chard in the boiling water, bring back to a boil and boil for 5 minutes. Remove from the heat, drain and squeeze excess water.
- Whisk the Tahini with the lemon juice, the pomegranate molasses, the water, the garlic, the cumin and the salt into smooth dressing.
- Pour the Tahini dressing over the Swiss chard, toss and serve.

Spinach Omelet

Serves 4

1 cup frozen chopped spinach, thawed
2 tablespoons olive oil
1 small onion, finely chopped
4 eggs
2 tablespoons grated Parmesan cheese
salt and pepper to taste

- Squeeze excess water from the spinach.
- Whisk the eggs lightly.
- Heat the oil in a non-stick frying pan. Stir in the onions and cook for a couple of minutes. Add the spinach, stir and cook for another couple of minutes.
- Pour in the eggs. Mix them quickly with the spinach and the seasoning. Cook the omelet over medium heat for 4 minutes or until puffed and golden.
- Place large plate over the omelet and gently turn the pan and the omelet over onto it. Slide the omelet back into the pan and cook until golden on the other side.
- Remove from the heat, sprinkle with cheese and serve.

Mashed Potato and Scallion Omelet

Serves 4

4 eggs
1 potato, boiled, peeled and mashed
2 scallions, finely chopped
1 clove garlic, mashed
2 tablespoons olive oil
salt and pepper to taste

- Whisk the eggs and then fold in the rest of the ingredients, except for the olive oil.
- Heat the oil in a non-stick frying pan. Pour in the egg mixture and cook over medium-low heat until omelet is puffed and golden. Turn the omelet over and cook the other side until golden. Serve.

Spicy Potatoes

Serves 4

4 medium potatoes
2 tablespoons olive oil
½ cup tomato sauce
¼ cup Tabasco sauce
1 teaspoon mustard
salt to taste

- Peel the potatoes, cut into 1-inch cubes and wash.
- Pat dry the potatoes, and then toss them with the olive oil.
- Bake in a 375 degree oven until golden. Remove from the oven and sprinkle with the salt.
- Whisk the tomato sauce with the Tabasco sauce and the mustard. Drizzle the hot sauce over the hot potatoes and serve.

Garbanzo Bean Spread (Hummous)

Makes 3 cups

3 cups garbanzo beans, cooked
(save 2 cups of the cooking liquid)
¼ cup Tahini*
2 cloves garlic
¼ cup lemon juice
¼ teaspoon ground cumin
salt to taste

- Place garbanzo beans, cooking liquid and garlic in a food processor. Process the beans until you have a smooth paste.
- Add the rest of the ingredients and process until well mixed. Taste the hummos and adjust seasoning before emptying into a serving bowl. Decorate with a little paprika and black pepper and serve.

Garbanzo Bean Dip with Parsley

Makes 3 cups

2 cups hummous (see recipe on page 26)
1 cup parsley, finely chopped
¼ cup lemon juice
3 tablespoons water
1 teaspoon ground cumin
salt to taste

- In a small bowl, mix all ingredients, then place in chilled serving bowl and serve.

Garbanzo Beans with Tahini Sauce

Serves 4

2 cups garbanzo beans, cooked
½ cup Tahini*
½ cup lemon juice
2 cloves garlic, mashed
1 teaspoon ground cumin
¼ cup parsley, finely chopped
salt to taste

- Whisk Tahini with lemon juice, garlic, ground cumin and salt.
- Place beans in a saucepan, add one cup of water and a dash of salt. Bring to a boil. Simmer for 5 minutes. Remove from heat and pour in a serving bowl.
- Pour the Tahini sauce over the beans, sprinkle with the chopped parsley and serve.

Roasted Winter Vegetables

Serves 4

- 1 medium sweet potato, peeled and cut into 1-inch cubes
- 2 medium potatoes, peeled and cut into 1-inch cubes
- 2 medium parsnips, peeled and cut into 1-inch cubes
- 2 red bell peppers, seeds removed and cut into 1-inch thick slices
- 4 tablespoons sesame oil
- 1 tablespoon balsamic vinegar
- 1 teaspoon ground cinnamon
- ½ teaspoon salt

- Heat oven to 450 degrees.
- Place the vegetables in a bowl. Mix the sesame oil with the vinegar, cinnamon and salt.
- Spread the vegetables out in a baking pan in one layer. Roast in the oven for 40 minutes or until golden and fork tender, then serve.

Sweet and Sour Beet Dip

Serves 4

4 beets
4 tablespoons Tahini*
2 cloves garlic, mashed
¼ cup lemon juice
salt to taste

- Boil the beets until tender. Remove from heat, peel and mash into a smooth paste.
- Add the rest of the ingredients and blend well, then serve.

Black Olive Spread

Makes 3 cups

2 cups pitted black cured olives or pitted Kalamata olives
1 cup walnuts, finely chopped
½ lemon, coarsely chopped with the skin
½ cup fresh oregano leaves
¼ cup olive oil
salt and pepper to taste

- Place all ingredients in a food processor.
- Using about five on/off turns, process until mixture is chopped finely, but not pureed. Serve.

Green Olive Spread

Makes 4 cups

2 cups green olives, pitted
2 cups walnuts, finely chopped
1 cup sweet onion, chopped
1 cup parsley, chopped
1 tablespoon pickled jalapeno, sliced
1 teaspoon dry oregano
¼ cup lemon juice
½ cup olive oil
salt to taste

- Place all ingredients in a food processor.
- Using the on/off button, process until mixture is chopped finely, but not pureed, then serve.

Garbanzo Bean Patties (Falafel)

Makes 40 patties

8 ounces dry garbanzo beans
1 small onion, finely chopped
1 cup parsley, finely chopped
1 tablespoon ground coriander
1 tablespoon ground cumin
1 teaspoon baking powder
oil for deep frying
salt and pepper to taste

- Soak the beans in cold water for 8 hours. Drain the beans and place in a food processor. Using the on/off button, process until the beans are coarsely chopped.
- Add parsley and onion to the beans and process until mixture is chopped finely, but not pureed.
- Spoon mixture into a large bowl. Add seasoning and mix well.
- Stir in the baking powder just before frying.
- Shape the mixture into patties two-inches in diameter and two-inches thick. Deep fry in hot oil until well-browned. Remove from oil and place on a plate lined with a paper towel.
- Serve with Tahini Yogurt Sauce (see recipe on page 34).

Tahini Yogurt Sauce

Makes 4 cups

3 cups plain yogurt
½ cup Tahini*
½ cup lemon juice
½ teaspoon ground cumin
salt to taste

• In a glass bowl, whisk all ingredients into a smooth sauce. Serve as a sauce for falafel, or on seafood.

Vegetarian Stuffed Grape Leaves

Makes about 40 grape leaves

1 16-ounce can of grape leaves,
drained and washed a couple of times.
2 cups short grain rice
1 medium onion, finely chopped
1 cup parsley, finely chopped
6 cloves garlic, mashed
2 medium tomatoes, finely chopped
1 cup olive oil
1 cup lemon juice
1 teaspoon allspice
1 large potato
salt and pepper to taste

- In a pan, sauté the onions in two cups of olive oil until translucent. Add the rice, stir and cook for 1 minute. Add 12 cups of water, stir and cook over medium heat until water is well absorbed.
- Remove from the heat and stir in the parsley, tomatoes, garlic, one-fourth cup lemon juice, allspice, salt and pepper. Stir well.
- Place one grape leaf on a flat surface. Place one tablespoon of rice stuffing in the center of the rough side of the leaf. Fold the stem side horizontally over the stuffing, then fold the two vertical sides over the first fold; roll tightly until it reaches the leaf point, forming a cylinder three-inches long by 1-inch thick. What is important, is that you fold the ends in before rolling so the stuffing does not come out.

(Continued on next page)

- Peel the potato and cut into ½-inch thick slices. Line the bottom of a large pan with the potatoes. The potatoes will prevent any sticking.
- Place grape leaf rolls side by side over the potatoes. When you finish the first layer of the stuffed leaves; drizzle a couple of tablespoons of olive oil on top, then arrange the rest of the stuffed leaves on the top of the first layer, until you have layered all the leaves.
- On top of the final layer, pour the rest of the olive oil, salt and then, place a flat plate on top of the rolls, which prevents the rolls from floating upward.
- Pour in about four cups of water or until you have about 1-inch of water over the plate.
- Place pot on the stove and bring to a boil. Taste the water to adjust salt, then turn heat to medium-low and simmer for 45 minutes.
- Remove the plate, drizzle lemon juice over the rolls and turn off the heat.
- Allow the rolls to cool completely, then place a round shallow platter over the top of the cooking pot and turn it upside down. Wait a couple of minutes before removing the pot. Remove the potatoes and serve. Refrigerated, these rolls taste better the next day and can keep for a week.

Zucchini Fritters

Makes 20 fritters

2 zucchini, finely chopped
1 small onion, finely chopped
1 cup feta cheese, crumbled
½ cup parsley, finely chopped
1 teaspoon dry mint
3 eggs, lightly beaten
1 cup white sorghum flour
olive oil for frying
salt and pepper to taste

- Mix zucchini, onion, feta, parsley and mint. Add eggs, salt and pepper. Stir, then add the flour, mix well.
- Heat the olive oil in a frying pan, drop a tablespoonful of the zucchini batter into the oil, and don't crowd the oil. Fry until golden on one side, then turn and fry the other side until it is also golden.
- Using a slotted spoon, remove the fritters to a flat dish lined with a paper towel to absorb the excess oil. Serve hot or cold.

Baked Tomatoes

Serves 4

4 medium tomatoes, not overripe and sliced in half
3 cloves garlic, mashed
¼ cup cilantro, finely chopped
3 tablespoons tomato juice
2 tablespoons olive oil
¼ cup slivered almonds, toast and coarsely grind
salt and fresh ground pepper to taste

- Preheat oven to 400 degrees.
- Place the tomatoes, cut side up, in a baking dish and sprinkle with some salt.
- Mix garlic, cilantro, salt and tomato juice.
- Spoon the garlic mixture on top of the tomatoes, drizzle with olive oil, then sprinkle with the ground almond.
- Bake for 30 minutes and serve.

Roasted Summer Vegetables

Serves 8

2 large eggplants
4 red bell peppers
2 yellow bell peppers
¼ cup olive oil
3 cloves garlic, mashed
¼ cup black olives, finely chopped
salt and pepper to taste

- Roast or grill the vegetables until skin is well charred. Remove and place in a large paper bag for 15-30 minutes.
- Peel the peppers, seed and cut into thin slices. Place in a bowl.
- Peel the eggplants, trim the stalks and cut into thin slices. Add to the peppers.
- Mix olive oil and garlic with salt and pepper, then drizzle over the vegetables. Toss gently and place in a shallow serving platter.
- Sprinkle with the chopped olives and serve.

Cheese Toast

Serves 5

1 basic pizza dough (see recipe on page 184)
6 tablespoons olive oil
8 ounces goat cheese
1 cup ricotta cheese
1 tablespoon fresh thyme, chopped
4 tablespoons olive oil

- Cut the half-baked pizza dough into 2-inch squares. Arrange the squares on a cookie sheet, then drizzle with two tablespoons of olive oil.
- Place in a 400 degree oven and bake for a couple of minutes. Remove from the oven.
- Cream the goat cheese with the ricotta cheese. Spread the cheese on top of the squares.
- Drizzle the rest of the olive oil on top of cheese and broil until the cheese is golden. Remove from the oven.
- Sprinkle with thyme and serve hot or at room temperature.

Artichokes with Asparagus Stuffing

Serves 4

4 small artichokes
8 medium asparagus spears
3 tablespoons olive oil
½ cup fresh or frozen peas, thaw frozen peas
2 tablespoons soy flour
½ cup heavy cream
1 clove garlic, mashed
¼ teaspoon freshly ground nutmeg
1 teaspoon tarragon
salt and pepper to taste

- In a large saucepan, bring salted water to a boil. Cut the top one third off each artichoke, then drop them in the boiling water and boil for 20 minutes.
- Remove the artichokes and allow to cool slightly. Cut each artichoke in half lengthwise. Remove the hairy chokes and a couple of the inner leaves, then place the artichokes in a baking tray, cut side up.
- Cut the asparagus into 1-inch wide pieces. Heat two tablespoons olive oil in a saucepan and cook the asparagus over low heat for 5 minutes. Add the peas and cook for another 5 minutes.
- Spoon the asparagus and pea mixture inside the artichokes.
- In a heavy saucepan, heat the rest of the olive oil and blend the flour into a smooth paste. Add the heavy cream, garlic, tarragon, nutmeg and salt. Whisk and

(Continued on next page)

cook over medium heat for 5 minutes or until the sauce slightly thickens. Remove from heat.

- Spoon the cream mixture on top of the asparagus and pea mixture.
- Bake in a 375 degree oven for 20 minutes. Remove and serve hot.

Garbanzo Filled Tomatoes

Serves 6

6 large plum tomatoes
1 cup garbanzo beans, cooked and mashed
3 scallions, chopped
2 garlic cloves, mashed
2 cups parsley, finely chopped
5 tablespoons vinegar
4 tablespoons olive oil
salt and pepper to taste

- Wash the tomatoes and cut in half lengthwise, remove the seeds and salt inside lightly.
- Place tomatoes cut side down on a towel and let them sit for 10 minutes.
- Mix ground garbanzo beans, garlic and parsley with the chopped scallions, olive oil and salt. Mix well and adjust seasoning.
- Fill the tomatoes with this mixture and place on a shallow serving platter. Refrigerate for 30 minutes. Serve.

Gorgonzola Cheese Canapés

Serves 6

12 2-inch thick olive bread slices, (see recipe on page 175)
2 tablespoons gluten free ricotta cheese (see recipe on page 172)
1 cup Gorgonzola cheese, soften and mashed into a smooth paste
1 tablespoon lemon juice
2 scallions, chopped
1 tomato, seeded and finely diced

- Toast the bread slices until crispy.
- Whip the ricotta cheese until creamy.
- Add the Gorgonzola cheese, lemon juice and scallions.
- Spread the mixture on the bread. Place on a serving platter, sprinkle with the diced tomatoes and serve.

Fragrant Peppers

Serves 6

- 4 yellow bell peppers
- ⅓ cup capers, drained
- 1 clove garlic, mashed
- ½ cup parsley, finely chopped
- ½ cup black olives, finely chopped
- 2 tablespoons Tabasco sauce
- 3 tablespoons Worcestershire sauce
- 1 teaspoon mustard
- 4 tablespoons olive oil

- Cut the peppers in halves, place on a cookie sheet and broil until charred.
- Remove from the oven, place in a paper bag, close and cool for awhile.
- Remove the peppers from the bag and remove the charred skins and seeds. Cut into 1-inch wide slices.
- Whisk Tabasco sauce, Worcestershire sauce, mustard, garlic and olive oil. Pour this dressing over the peppers, cover and let stand for at least 1 hour.
- Finely chop capers and black olives, then mix and sprinkle this mixture over the peppers before serving.

Baby Onions with Wine

Serves 6-8

1 pound pearl onions, peeled
3 tablespoons butter
1 clove garlic, mashed
½ cup wine
2 tablespoons sugar
1 tablespoon white wine vinegar

- In a large saucepan, bring salted water to a boil. Drop in the onions, bring back to boil and let boil for 5 minutes. Drain the onions and set aside.
- In a shallow frying pan, melt the butter and sauté the garlic for a few seconds. Add the onions, stir gently and cook the onions until golden brown, moving the pan continuously.
- Add the wine, sugar and white vinegar. Cover and cook until the liquid evaporates. Remove from heat and serve.

Pickled Mushrooms

Serves 4

1 pound small white mushrooms
¼ cup lemon juice
¼ cup olive oil
1 cup white vinegar
½ cup fresh tarragon
1 fresh jalapeno pepper, diced
salt to taste

- Clean and remove the stems from the mushrooms.
- Mix the vinegar with the oil, tarragon, jalapeno pepper and salt in a saucepan and bring to a boil. Remove from heat and set aside.
- Bring salted water to a boil. Add the mushrooms and lemon juice. Simmer for 5 minutes. Drain and place in a large glass jar or container. Pour the hot vinegar solution over the mushrooms. Close tight and allow mushrooms to marinate for a week before serving.

Olive Relish with Coriander

Makes 2 cups

1 12-ounce jar pitted green olives
½ cup celery, finely chopped
½ cup pistachios, toasted
¼ cup olive oil
¼ cup vinegar
1 clove garlic, mashed
1 teaspoon ground coriander
¼ teaspoon ground cumin

- Chop olives finely and toss with the diced celery and the pistachio.
- Mix olive oil, vinegar, garlic, coriander and cumin, then add to the olives and mix. Cover and refrigerate overnight. Serve.

Tomato and Basil Bruschetta

Makes 8 pieces

8 slices, ½-inch thick olive bread
  (see recipe page 181)
2 medium ripe tomatoes, diced
1 cup fresh basil, finely chopped
4 tablespoons olive oil
1 clove garlic, mashed
  salt to taste

- Mix two tablespoons olive oil, garlic and salt.
- Place bread slices on a cookie sheet and toast for a couple of minutes.
- Remove from the oven and cool.
- Toss the diced tomatoes with the basil and the remaining olive oil, then spoon on top of the toasted bread. Serve.

Green Pepper Tapenade

Makes 2 cups

1 green bell pepper, chopped
2 green jalapeno peppers, seeded and chopped
1 Serrano pepper, seeded and chopped
1 cup parsley, chopped
1 cup cilantro, chopped
½ cup walnuts
¼ cup olive oil
¼ cup lemon juice
zest of one lemon
salt to taste

- Place all ingredients in a food processor.
- Process into a smooth paste, but not a mushy paste, by using the on/off button.

SOUPS

Lentil Soup

Serves 4-6

1 pound lentils
2 carrots, finely chopped
2 stalks celery, finely chopped
1 medium onion, finely chopped
3 tablespoons olive oil
1 16-ounce can tomato sauce
1 teaspoon sage
2 bay leaves
1 clove garlic
salt to taste

- In a heavy soup pot, heat the olive oil and sauté the onions for a couple of minutes.
- Add the celery and the carrots—this will make a *roux*. Stir and cook over medium-low heat for 5 minutes.
- Add the lentils and ten cups of water, bay leaves, sage, garlic and salt. Bring to a boil. Boil until lentils are soft, but not mushy.
- Add the tomato sauce and bring back to a boil. Simmer for 10 minutes. Serve hot.

Lentil Cilantro Soup

Serves 4-6

1 pound lentils
4 tablespoons olive oil
1 medium onion, julienned
6 cloves garlic, mashed
1 cup cilantro, chopped
¼ cup lemon juice
1 cup gluten-free elbow pasta
salt to taste

- In a soup pot, heat olive oil and cook the onions until golden.
- Add the lentils, eight cups of water and bring to a boil. Boil until lentils are soft, but not mushy.
- In a small pan, heat the rest of the olive oil and sauté the garlic with the cilantro for 1 minute, then add the lemon juice.
- Add the cilantro lemon mixture to the soup. Adjust the seasoning, then drop in the pasta. Stir and cook for 5 minutes and serve.

Cream of Split Pea Soup

Serves 6-8

8 ounces split peas
4 tablespoons olive oil
1 small onion, finely chopped
2 celery stalks, finely chopped
3 carrots, finely chopped
2 small potatoes, peeled and diced into half-inch cubes
2 cloves garlic, chopped
½ cup cilantro, chopped
½ cup lemon juice
salt and pepper to taste

- In a heavy pot, heat olive oil, then cook the onions with the celery and carrots for 5 minutes.
- Add the peas, potatoes and eight cups of water. Bring to a boil.
- Boil the soup for 1 hour. Add garlic, cilantro, salt and pepper, and simmer for 1 hour.
- Remove from heat, puree into a smooth soup. Serve with corn chips.

Vegetable Soup

Serves 6-8

3 tablespoons olive oil
1 medium onion, chopped
2 celery stalks, diced
3 carrots, diced
1 zucchini, diced
2 medium potatoes, peeled and diced
1 cup cabbage, chopped
1 cup kale, chopped
1 16-ounce can diced tomatoes
1 16-ounce can cooked kidney beans
1 teaspoon sage
2 bay leaves
½ cup Parmesan cheese
salt and pepper to taste

- In a heavy pot, heat the olive oil and sauté the onion, celery and carrots for a couple of minutes.
- Add the diced tomatoes with the juice, eight cups of water, sage, bay leaves, salt and pepper. Bring to a boil, then add the kale, cabbage and zucchini. Bring back to a boil. Turn down the heat and cook over medium heat for 10 minutes. Add the potatoes and cook for 10 minutes or until the potatoes are done.
- Add the beans and the cheese, stir, adjust the seasoning and serve.

Roasted Red Bell Pepper and Wild Rice Soup

Serves 4-6

4 tablespoons olive oil
1 small onion, finely chopped
1 cup celery, chopped
1 cup carrots, chopped
1 cup wild rice
4 large red bell peppers
1 fresh fennel, julienned
8 ounces tomato sauce
½ teaspoon ground fennel seeds
salt and pepper to taste

- Boil wild rice until soft, but not mushy. Drain and set aside.
- Place the pepper on a baking sheet and broil until charred on both sides. Remove from the oven and place in a paper bag. Cool for 10 minutes. Remove from the bag and peel the charred skin and remove the seeds. Puree in a food processor.
- In a soup pot, heat the olive oil, then sauté the onions with the carrots and the celery. Stir and cook over low heat for 5 minutes. Add the julienned fennel, stir and cook for another minute.
- Add the pureed roasted pepper, tomato sauce, four cups of water and the seasoning. Cover and simmer for 5 minutes.
- Add the rice, stir and continue to simmer for another 5 minutes, then serve.

Potato Soup

Serves 4-6

2 large potatoes
6 cups water
1 medium onion, finely chopped
3 tablespoons olive oil
1 cup skim milk
2 cloves garlic, mashed
1 6-ounce can sliced mushrooms
½ teaspoon tarragon
½ teaspoon paprika
salt and pepper to taste

- Peel the potatoes and cut into 1-inch cubes.
- Place the potatoes in the water and add the tarragon, paprika and a little salt. Boil until the potatoes are very soft. Remove from the heat and puree until a smooth thick liquid.
- In a large heavy pot, sauté the onions in the olive oil for a couple of minutes. Add the garlic and the mushroom, stir and cook for 1 minute. Pour in the pureed potatoes, pepper, and the milk. Stir and simmer for 10 minutes or until the soup thickens, then serve.

Leek, Potato and White Bean Soup

Serves 4-6

4 tablespoons olive oil
1 medium onion, julienned
2 small leeks (use white part only), thinly sliced
½ cup fresh fennel, chopped (optional)
2 small potatoes, peeled and cut into 1-inch cubes
1 cup white cannelini beans, cooked
salt and pepper to taste

- In a heavy pot, heat olive oil and sauté the onions until golden.
- Add the leeks, fennels and potatoes, sauté for 5 minutes while stirring.
- Add six cups of water, vegetable bouillon, salt and pepper. Stir and bring to a boil. Cover and simmer for 30 minutes.
- Add the beans, adjust the seasoning and continue to simmer for 5 minutes. Remove from heat and serve.

Bean and Potato Soup

Serves 4-6

1 12-ounce can cooked kidney beans
4 tablespoons olive oil
2 cloves garlic, mashed
1 medium onion, finely chopped
1 celery stalk, finely chopped
3 medium potatoes, peeled and diced
2 medium ripe tomatoes, finely diced
4 cups gluten free vegetable broth
(see recipe on page 173)
½ teaspoon sage
2 bay leaves
1 cup parsley, chopped
¼ cup Parmesan cheese
salt and pepper to taste

- In a heavy pot, heat the olive oil and sauté the garlic, onion and celery for 5 minutes.
- Wash and drain the beans, save one cup of the beans for later and place the rest in the pot. Add the tomatoes, potatoes, and vegetable broth. Bring to a boil.
- Add the sage, bay leaves, half of the parsley, salt and pepper.
- Cover and simmer for 30 minutes, stirring from time to time.
- Remove from heat, discard the bay leaves and puree the soup in a food processor or blender.
- Return to the stove; add the beans saved earlier, and the Parmesan cheese. Stir, adjust the seasoning and cook for an additional 10 minutes. Serve.

Vegetable and Pasta Soup

Serves 4-6

4 tablespoons olive oil
1 medium onion, chopped
3 celery stalks, chopped
3 carrots, diced
1 clove garlic, mashed
1 32-ounce can tomato sauce
2 bay leaves
1 teaspoon dry sage
1 cup lentils
1 zucchini, diced
1 potato, peeled and diced
½ cup gluten-free elbow pasta
salt and pepper to taste

- In a heavy pot, heat olive oil and cook the onions for a couple of minutes.
- Add the celery and carrots, then sauté for 5 minutes while stirring.
- Add the garlic, tomato sauce, four cups of water, bay leaves, salt and pepper. Bring to a boil.
- Add the vegetables and lentils, bring back to a boil, then reduce the heat and simmer until lentils are soft.
- Adjust the seasoning and add the pasta, stir and cook until pasta is al-dente. You can add more water if the soup is little thick. Serve.

Chicken Soup

Serves 4-6

6 cups gluten free chicken broth (see recipe on page 175)
½ cup short grain rice
½ teaspoon tarragon
2 chicken breasts, cooked and cut into thin strips
¼ cup parsley, chopped
salt and pepper to taste

- In a heavy pot, bring broth to a boil.
- Add rice and tarragon, then simmer while stirring for 10-15 minutes or until rice is cooked, but not mushy.
- Add the chicken and bring back to a boil. Boil for 5 minutes.
- Remove from heat, stir in the parsley and serve.

Swiss Chard and Lentil Soup

Serves 4-6

2 cups lentils
4 tablespoons olive oil
1 medium onion, chopped
1 pound Swiss chard, chopped
2 tablespoons garbanzo bean flour
½ cup lemon juice
½ teaspoon cumin
salt and pepper to taste

- In a heavy soup pan, cover lentils with eight cups of water and cook for 20 minutes or until lentils are soft.
- In a frying pan, heat two tablespoons of olive oil, then sauté the onions for a couple of minutes. Add the Swiss chard, stir and cook over medium heat for 5 minutes. Add this mixture to the lentils.
- In the same frying pan, heat the rest of the olive oil. Add the flour and cumin and mix until you have a smooth paste. Stir in the lemon juice, then add to the soup.
- Add the salt and pepper and continue to cook, stirring often until soup thickens, then serve.

Garbanzo Bean Soup

Serves 4-6

4 tablespoons olive oil
1 medium onion, finely chopped
1 clove garlic
4 cups garbanzo beans, cooked
½ teaspoon oregano
½ teaspoon rosemary
1 cup short gluten-free pasta
½ cup Parmesan cheese
salt and pepper to taste

- Heat the olive oil and cook the onion for a couple of minutes.
- Add half of the garbanzo beans, eight cups of water, oregano, rosemary and salt. Bring to a boil.
- Puree the rest of the garbanzo beans and the garlic in a food processor. Add the puree to the boiling beans.
- Bring the soup back to a boil and adjust the seasoning.
- Stir in the pasta and cook until al-dente.
- Stir in the cheese and serve.

Spicy Garbanzo Bean Soup

Serves 6

5 cups garbanzo beans, cooked
2 tablespoons olive oil
1 medium onion, chopped
1 carrot, diced
2 celery stalks, diced
1 tablespoon Harissa*
1 cup chopped red cabbage
1 cup crushed tomatoes
1 teaspoon sage
1 bay leaf
salt and pepper to taste

- In a heavy soup pot, heat olive oil and cook the onion for 2 minutes. Add the carrots and celery. Stir and cook for 5 minutes.
- Add the Harissa and cabbage. Stir and cook for a couple of minutes.
- Add two cups of water, the crushed tomatoes, sage, bay leaf, salt and pepper. Stir and bring to a boil.
- Add half of the cooked garbanzo beans. Bring back to a boil and simmer for 10 minutes.
- Puree the rest of the garbanzo beans in a food processor and spoon into the simmering soup.
- Stir well, adjust seasoning and continue to simmer for 5 more minutes. Serve.

Cream of Zucchini Soup

Serves 4-6

2 tablespoons olive oil
1 medium onion, chopped
2 pounds zucchini, chopped
1 clove garlic, mashed
1 teaspoon nutmeg
½ teaspoon ground cloves
½ teaspoon mint
4 cups gluten free vegetable broth (see recipe on page 173)
1 cup evaporated skim milk
salt and pepper to taste

- Heat the olive oil and cook the onions for 5 minutes.
- Add the zucchini, stir and cook over medium heat for 10 minutes. Add the garlic, mint, cloves, nutmeg and the vegetable broth. Stir and continue cooking for another 10 minutes.
- Remove zucchini from heat and puree in a food processor until smooth.
- Return the zucchini to the pot. Add the rest of the seasoning and the evaporated skim milk. Stir and cook over low heat until hot. Serve.

Acorn Squash Soup

Serves 4

6 ounces lite tofu, drained
3 ounces leek
6 ounces acorn squash,
  peeled and cut into 1-inch cubes
1 small yam, peeled and cut into 1-inch cubes
2 cups water
2 tablespoons sesame seed oil
4 cups gluten free vegetable broth
  (see recipe on page 173)
½ teaspoon fresh ground nutmeg
2 cloves
  salt to taste

- Sauté the leek in the sesame seed oil over low heat for a couple of minutes.
- Add the rest of the vegetables and one cup of the water, stir and cook for 5 minutes.
- Add the tofu, seasoning, broth, and the water. Stir and bring to a boil. Cover and simmer for 20 minutes or until vegetables are soft.
- Remove the cloves, then puree the soup in a food processor until smooth.
- Return soup to the pot. Add water if the soup is very thick. Adjust the seasoning and cook over low heat for 5 more minutes. Serve.

Three Bean Soup

Serves 6

1 cup lentils
3 tablespoons olive oil
1 medium onion, chopped
1 celery stalk, chopped
1 clove garlic, mashed
1 red bell pepper, seeded and chopped
2 cups tomatoes, diced
1 cup garbanzo beans, cooked
1 cup black-eye peas, cooked
1 teaspoon ground cumin
½ teaspoon chili powder
salt to taste

- Heat the olive oil and sauté the onions until soft.
- Add the celery, garlic and both chopped peppers. Stir and cook over low heat for 5 minutes.
- Add the lentils and eight cups of water. Bring to a boil and cook until lentils are soft.
- Add the rest of the ingredients, stir and bring back to a boil. Cover and simmer for 10 minutes. Serve.

SALADS

Watercress and Mushroom Salad

Serves 4-6

2 bunches watercress
8 ounces white mushrooms, thinly sliced
¼ cup lemon juice
3 tablespoons olive oil
salt and pepper to taste

- Chop the watercress and toss with the mushrooms.
- Mix the lemon juice with the olive oil and seasoning. Pour the lemon dressing over the watercress and toss gently. Serve.

Mushroom and Scallion Salad

Serves 4

4 cups white mushrooms, sliced
2 cups scallions, chopped
½ cup fresh cilantro, chopped
½ cup lemon juice
¼ cup olive oil
½ teaspoon basil
salt and pepper to taste

- Mix the scallions with the mushrooms and cilantro.
- Whisk the basil with the lemon juice, olive oil, salt and pepper. Drizzle over the salad mixture. Toss gently and serve.

Romaine Lettuce and Garbanzo Bean Salad

Serves 4

10 leaves romaine lettuce, chopped
1 bunch parsley, chopped
4 scallions, chopped
2 medium tomatoes, diced
1 cucumber, diced
½ cup quinoa
1 cup garbanzo beans, cooked
¼ cup lemon juice
¼ cup olive oil
salt to taste

- In a saucepan, bring one cup of water with one tablespoon of oil to a boil. Drop in the quinoa and cook for a couple of minutes.
- Turn off the heat and set aside to cool at room temperature. Squeeze any excess water from the quinoa and place in a salad bowl.
- Toss vegetables with the beans and quinoa.
- Whisk the oil with lemon juice and salt. Drizzle over the vegetables, toss and serve.

Cabbage and Radish Salad

Serves 4

2 cups green cabbage, chopped
1 cup red cabbage, chopped
1 cup radishes, chopped
1 cup carrots, chopped
½ cup dried cranberries
1 teaspoon mint
⅓ cup lemon juice
4 tablespoons olive oil
½ cup roasted sunflower seeds
salt and pepper to taste

• Toss all ingredients and serve.

Tomato and Scallion Salad

Serves 4

3 medium tomatoes, diced
6 scallions, chopped
1 cup fresh oregano, chopped
½ cup feta cheese, crumbled
3 tablespoons lemon juice
4 tablespoons olive oil
zest of one lemon
salt and pepper to taste

- Gently toss tomatoes with scallions and oregano.
- Whisk lemon juice, lemon zest, olive oil and seasoning. Drizzle over the vegetables and toss.
- Sprinkle the feta cheese on top and serve.

Cucumber with Feta Cheese and Oregano Salad

Serves 4

6 small pickling cucumbers
2 cups fresh oregano, chopped
1 medium sweet onion, julienne
1 cup feta cheese, crumbled
2 tablespoons vinegar
4 tablespoons olive oil

• Toss ingredients together and serve.

Caprese Salad

Serves 4

2 large ripe tomatoes, sliced
4 ounces fresh mozzarella, sliced
½ cup fresh basil, chopped
¼ cup Kalamata olives, chopped
2 tablespoons olive oil
fresh ground black pepper

- On a flat serving platter, arrange the cheese in one layer. Arrange the tomato slices on top of the cheese.
- Sprinkle the basil and the olives on top of the tomatoes.
- Drizzle the oil over the vegetables.
- Sprinkle with black pepper and serve.

Mediterranean Potato Salad

Serves 4

3 medium potatoes, boiled
1 medium tomato, finely diced
1 medium sweet onion, finely chopped
1 clove garlic, mashed
4 tablespoons olive oil
2 tablespoons lemon juice
zest of one lemon
salt to taste

- Peel and dice the potatoes into half-inch cubes.
- Toss the potatoes with the vegetables.
- Add the olive oil, lemon zest, lemon juice and salt. Toss gently and serve.

Potato and Roasted Pepper Salad

Serves 4

½ pound baby new potatoes
½ cup capers
2 red bell peppers
1 yellow bell pepper
1 jalapeno pepper
2 tablespoons mustard
4 tablespoons olive oil
4 tablespoons lemon juice
salt and pepper to taste

- Place the potatoes in a pot, bring to a boil and boil until the potatoes are cooked. Remove from the heat, rinse with cold water and cut in halves.
- Place peppers on a cookie sheet and broil until charred. Remove from the oven, place in a paper bag and seal. Allow the peppers to cool in the bag.
- Remove the peppers from the bag; remove the skin and seeds.
- Chop the peppers coarsely. Set aside.
- Gently toss the potatoes with the roasted peppers and the caper.
- Whisk the olive oil with the lemon juice, mustard, thyme, salt and pepper. Drizzle this dressing over the potato mixture and toss gently.
- Cover the salad and refrigerate for at least 1 hour before serving.

Spinach and Walnut Salad

Serves 4

5 cups fresh baby spinach
1 cup walnuts, coarsely chopped and toasted
½ cup dried cranberries
¼ cup feta cheese, crumbled
3 tablespoons olive oil
2 tablespoons lemon juice
fresh ground black pepper

- Toss the spinach with the walnuts and cranberries.
- Drizzle the olive oil and the lemon juice over the salad and toss gently.
- Sprinkle the cheese and the pepper on top of the salad and serve.

Bean Salad

Serves 6

1 cup garbanzo beans, cooked
1 cup kidney beans, cooked
1 cup corn, cooked
½ cup black beans, cooked
1 red bell pepper, finely diced
½ cup parsley, chopped
4 scallions, finely diced
¼ cup olive oil
3 tablespoons lemon juice
salt to taste

- Toss beans and vegetables together.
- Add the oil, lemon juice and salt. Toss and serve.

Cucumber and Yogurt Salad

Serves 4

2 cups plain non-fat yogurt
½ cup water
2 small pickling cucumbers, finely diced
1 clove garlic, mashed
1 teaspoon dry mint
salt to taste

- Whisk yogurt, water, garlic, mint and salt into a smooth paste
- Add the cucumbers mix. Serve cold.

Bread Salad

Serves 4

2 loaves of flat bread, (see recipe on page 173)
1 tablespoon dry thyme
1 medium tomato, diced
1 medium cucumber, peeled and diced
2 scallions, diced
2 radishes, julienne
1 cup parsley, chopped
4 Romaine lettuce leaves, chopped
¼ cup olive oil
4 tablespoons lemon juice
½ teaspoon dry mint
1 tablespoon sesame seeds
zest of one lemon
salt to taste

- Mix thyme, mint, salt and sesame seeds with two tablespoons of olive oil. Brush this mixture on the bread. Toast the bread in a 375 degree oven until golden. Remove from the oven and leave the bread to cool. Cut the bread into small pieces. Set aside.
- Whisk together olive oil, lemon zest and salt to make the dressing.
- In a salad bowl, toss all the vegetables, then drizzle the dressing over the vegetables. Toss until well coated.
- Sprinkle the toasted thyme bread over the salad and serve.

Corn Couscous and Broccoli Salad

Serves 4

1 cup quinoa
2 cups broccoli floret
1 cup carrots, shredded
1 red bell pepper, diced
½ cup raisins
¼ cup sunflower seeds, toasted
½ cup lemon juice
¼ cup sesame seeds oil
zest of one lemon
salt to taste

- Bring two cups of salted water to a boil. Add the quinoa and one tablespoon of sesame oil. Stir and bring back to a boil. Cook for 5 minutes. Remove from heat and allow the quinoa to set for 10 minutes. Squeeze excess water from the quinoa.
- Add the rest of the ingredients, toss and serve warm or cold.

Wild Rice Salad

Serves 4

1 cup wild rice
½ cup carrots, shredded
1 cup red cabbage, shredded
1 cup green cabbage, shredded
½ cup toasted walnuts, chopped and toasted
½ cup dried cranberries
4 tablespoons walnut oil
6 tablespoons lemon juice
1 tablespoon honey
zest of one lemon

- Boil wild rice until soft, but not mushy. Drain and toss with one tablespoon of walnut oil and one tablespoon of lemon juice.
- Mix the vegetables and dried cranberries with the wild rice.
- Whisk together the remaining walnut oil with the lemon juice, honey, lemon juice and lemon zest. Drizzle over the vegetable mixture. Toss well.
- Sprinkle the toasted walnuts on top and serve.

Garbanzo Bean and Mint Salad with Quinoa

Serves 6

1 cup quinoa
1 cup garbanzo beans, cooked
2 baby cucumbers, diced
2 scallions, chopped
1 cup fresh mint, chopped
1 teaspoon black pepper
¼ cup olive oil
¼ cup lemon juice
zest of one lemon
salt to taste

- Bring one cup of water to a boil. Stir in the quinoa and cook for 5 minutes. Remove from heat, fluff and allow quinoa to cool.
- Squeeze excess water.
- Mix the vegetables with the beans and quinoa
- Whisk lemon juice with the olive oil, lemon zest and seasoning. Drizzle the lemon dressing over the vegetable salad. Add the fresh mint and toss well.

Tabouli Salad

Serves 4

2 bunches parsley, finely chopped
2 medium tomatoes, finely diced
1 small sweet onion, finely chopped
½ cup quinoa
¼ cup olive oil
½ cup lemon juice
salt to taste

- Bring a half cup of water to a boil, drop in the quinoa, stir and cook for 5 minutes. Remove from heat and allow the quinoa to cool.
- Squeeze excess water from the quinoa, then add the vegetables and toss gently.
- Add olive oil, lemon juice and salt. Toss until well coated and serve.

Spinach Salad with Beets and Clementine Oranges

Serves 4

4 cups baby spinach
1 beet
2 Clementine oranges, peeled and sectioned
1 cup almonds, slivered and toasted
2 tablespoons lemon juice
4 tablespoons olive oil
salt and pepper to taste

- Boil the beet until tender. Remove from heat, rinse with cold water and peel. Cut into 1-inch cubes.
- Place the spinach in a salad bowl. Scatter the Clementine oranges and the beets over the spinach.
- Whisk the lemon juice, olive oil, mustard, salt and pepper. Drizzle this dressing over the spinach and toss gently.
- Sprinkle with the toasted almonds and serve.

Nicoise Salad

Serves 4-6

- ½ pound small potatoes, boiled
- ½ pound green beans, trimmed
- 2 hard-boiled eggs, quartered
- 1 head Boston lettuce, torn into bite-size pieces
- 2 medium tomatoes, cut into 8 wedges
- 12 ounces canned tuna, drained
- ½ cup Nicoise olives, (pitted Kalamata olives would be a good substitute)
- 4 tablespoons lemon juice
- 2 teaspoons Dijon mustard
- 4 tablespoons olive oil
- salt and pepper to taste

- To make the dressing; whisk lemon juice with the mustard, oil, salt and pepper.
- Place the potatoes in a pot, cover the potatoes with slightly salted water and bring to a boil. Simmer until the potatoes are tender. Remove from the heat, drain, rinse with cold water and peel.
- Cut the potatoes in halves and toss with one tablespoon of the dressing.
- Bring two quarts of water to a boil. Drop in the beans and cook for 5 minutes. Drain and rinse in cold water. Toss the beans with one tablespoon of the dressing.
- Spread the lettuce in a clear glass salad bowl. Scatter the potatoes and the beans over the lettuce.

(Continued on next page)

- Sprinkle the diced tomatoes on top of the potato layer, then top with the tuna.
- Arrange the boiled eggs on the edge of the salad bowl.
- Drizzle the rest of the salad dressing on top, then scatter the olives on top and serve.

Tuna Salad

Serves 4

12 ounces canned tuna chunks
4 celery stalks, diced
1 red onion, finely diced
2 cups olives, chopped
½ cup pickled cucumber, finely diced
1 cup green salsa
2 tablespoons olive oil

- Toss the vegetables with the tuna and the olives.
- Mix the green salsa with the olive oil, then gently mix with the tuna mixture, and serve.

Curly Endive Salad

Serves 4

1 bunch curly endive, chopped
1 tablespoon olive oil
¼ cup lemon juice
4 cloves garlic, mashed
salt to taste

- Bring a deep pot of water to a boil.
- Drop in the chopped endive and let it boil for 5 minutes. Remove from heat, drain and rinse with cold water.
- Squeeze out excess water and place in a serving bowl.
- Mix garlic, lemon juice, olive oil and salt. Drizzle this dressing over the endive and toss until well coated.
- Serve at room temperature.

MAIN DISHES

Lentil and Rice Pilaf

Serves 4-6

2 cups lentils
1 cup rice
¼ cup olive oil
2 medium onions, julienne
½ teaspoon ground cumin
salt to taste

- Heat the olive oil, then cook the onions in the oil until golden brown.
- Remove half of the onions and set aside. Add the lentils and eight cups of water along with the salt and cumin. Bring to a boil and cook until lentils are done, but still firm.
- Drain the lentils and the onion mixture into a pot. Save the cooking liquid. Measure 2¼ cup of the cooking liquid over the lentils. Bring back to a boil.
- Add the rice, stir and bring to a boil again.
- Cover and cook over low heat for 20 minutes. Turn off the heat and allow the rice to rest for 10 minutes.
- Scope the lentil rice pilaf into a shallow serving platter. Spread the rest of the caramelized onions on top and serve. It is best served with the yogurt cucumber salad.

Greek Eggplant Mousakaa

Serves 4

2 1-pound eggplants
2 medium onions, julienne
¼ cup olive oil
2 cloves garlic, thinly sliced
1 red bell pepper
1 32-ounce can diced tomatoes
salt and pepper to taste

- Slice the eggplants into half-inch thick slices. Place the eggplant slices on a cookie sheet, spray with olive oil spray and broil until golden brown. Turn to the other side, spray and broil until golden. Remove from the oven and set aside.
- Broil the pepper until charred on all sides. Place the pepper in a paper bag and seal. When the pepper is cold, remove from the bag, peel the skin and remove the seeds, then cut into thin slices.
- In a heavy pot, heat the olive oil and cook the onions until caramelized. Add the garlic and cook for 1 minute. Add the diced tomatoes, salt and pepper. Stir and cook for 5 minutes. Remove from heat.
- Remove half of the tomato onion mix and set it aside. Place the eggplants and the broiled pepper on top of the remaining mix, then spoon the rest of the tomato onion sauce on top of that. Cover and cook over medium-low heat for 25 minutes. Serve.

Chicken with Sesame Paste Sauce

Serves 4-6

1 pound of chicken breasts
8 ounces corn chips
1 cup rice, cooked
1 cup plain non-fat yogurt
4 tablespoons Tahini*
4 cloves garlic, mashed
¼ cup lemon juice
½ cup water
1 teaspoon ground cumin
2 tablespoons pine nuts, toasted
salt to taste

• Place chicken breasts with water, salt and pepper in a pot and bring to a boil. Boil until the chicken is done. Remove chicken breasts from the boiling chicken stock, cut into 1-inch pieces and put the pieces back in the pot with the chicken stock.

To make the sauce:

• Mix Tahini with garlic, lemon juice, cumin and salt. Whisk until you have a smooth sauce.

To assemble the dish:

• Place the corn chips in a 4-inch deep serving platter. Sprinkle the cooked rice over the chips, then put the chicken pieces on top of the rice. Drizzle on about a cup of the hot chicken stock. Spread the Tahini sauce on top of the chicken and chips. Cover evenly, sprinkle with pine nuts and serve.

Kufta (Seasoned Beef Balls) with Potatoes in Tomato Sauce

Serves 4

1½ pounds lean ground beef
1 medium onion, finely chopped
1 cup parsley, finely chopped
1 teaspoon allspice
2 tablespoons olive oil
2 cloves garlic, chopped
2 medium onions, julienne
2 medium potatoes, peeled and sliced into ½-inch thick slices
1 32-ounce can diced tomatoes
salt and pepper to taste

To make the kufta:

- Mix the beef with the parsley, onions, allspice, salt and pepper. Shape the meat into 2-inch balls, then flatten into half-inch thick patties. Set aside.
- In a heavy pot, heat the olive oil and sear the garlic for a few seconds. Add the onions and sauté for 5 minutes. Add the diced tomatoes with the juice, two cups of water and the seasoning. Bring back to a boil. Simmer for 10 minutes or until potatoes are about half done.

- Place the beef patties in a baking dish. Scoop the potatoes and onions on top, then pour in the remaining tomato sauce.
- Bake in a 395 degree oven for 35-45 minutes.

Kufta (Seasoned Beef Balls) with Three Pepper Sauce

Serves 4

1 pound ground beef
1 medium onion, finely chopped
1 cup parsley, chopped
1 clove garlic, mashed
½ teaspoon allspice
2 tablespoons olive oil
2 cloves garlic, sliced into thin slices
1 large onion, julienne
1 green bell pepper, julienne
1 red bell pepper, julienne
1 yellow bell pepper, julienne
1 16-ounce can diced tomatoes
½ teaspoon oregano
salt and pepper to taste

- Mix beef with the onion, parsley, garlic, allspice, salt and pepper. Divide the beef mix into 20 balls. Place on a plate and refrigerate.
- In a pot, heat the olive oil and sear the sliced garlic for a few seconds. Add the onions, stir and cook for a couple of minutes.
- Add the julienne peppers, stir and cook over low heat for 5 minutes.
- Add the diced tomatoes, oregano, salt and pepper. Bring to a boil.
- Adjust the seasoning, then drop in the beef balls. Simmer on medium-low heat for 15 minutes. Serve with rice.

Kufta Kebab with Yogurt Mint Sauce

Serves 4

- 1 pound ground beef
- 1 medium onion, finely chopped
- ½ cup parsley, finely chopped
- ½ teaspoon allspice
- 1 cup plain yogurt
- 1 clove garlic, mashed
- ½ teaspoon mint
- 8 wooden skewers
- salt and pepper to taste

To make the yogurt sauce:

- Whisk yogurt with the garlic, mint and salt. Chill until used.

- In a chilled bowl, mix the ground beef with the onion, parsley, allspice, salt and pepper.
- Divide the beef mixture into eight balls.
- Push a skewer through each beef ball. Holding the skewer⅔with one hand, with the other hand flatten the beef ball so that it becomes a long tube that covers of the skewer, about five-inches long.
- Broil or grill until done on both sides. Remove from the grill.
- Remove kebab from the skewer, then place each kebab on flat corn rice bread. Drizzle with the yogurt sauce and serve.

Eggplant Stuffed with Beef in Tomato Sauce

Serves 4

2 large eggplants
4 tablespoons olive oil
8 ounces lean ground beef
1 medium onion, chopped
1 15-ounce can diced tomatoes
1 tablespoon tomato paste
½ teaspoon allspice
½ teaspoon thyme
½ teaspoon rosemary
3 cups corn chips
¼ cup pine nuts, toasted, optional
salt and pepper to taste

- Peel and slice the eggplant into 1-inch thick slices. Place the eggplant on a cookie sheet. Spray with olive oil spray and broil until golden brown.
- Turn to the other side and broil until golden.
- In a pan, heat the olive oil and sauté the onions until transparent. Add the beef, allspice and salt. Stir and cook until meat is done.
- In a small soup pan, mix diced tomatoes with the tomato paste, thyme, rosemary and salt. Stir, bring to a boil and simmer for 5 minutes. Remove from heat.
- Arrange the chips in a baking tray, place the eggplant slices on top, then spread the beef stuffing on top of the eggplant.
- Pour the tomato sauce over the eggplant.

(Continued on next page)

- Bake in a 375 degree oven for 35 minutes. Remove from the oven, sprinkle with the toasted pine nuts and serve.

Eggplant Chicken Up-Side Down Mold

Serves 4-6

4 chicken breasts, cut into small pieces
1 large eggplant
4 tablespoons olive oil
2 cups short grain rice
½ teaspoon allspice
¼ teaspoon nutmeg
¼ cup almonds, slivered and toasted
salt and pepper to taste

- In a pot, boil the chicken in nine cups of water seasoned with allspice, nutmeg, salt and pepper. Boil until the chicken is done.
- Remove the chicken breasts and cut them into small pieces.
- Peel the eggplant, slice, spray with olive oil and broil until golden. Cut into small pieces. Set aside.
- In a heavy pot, place the chicken pieces in the oil and sear until golden. Remove from heat. Remove the chicken from the oil and set aside.
- Measure 4½ cups of the chicken broth, then pour over the oil and place back on the stove. Add the eggplant pieces.
- Bring to a boil, add the rice, stir and bring back to a boil. Cover and cook over very low heat for 25 minutes.
- In a greased mold, place the toasted almonds in the bottom of the mold. Place the chicken pieces in

(Continued on next page)

the mold over the nuts. Spoon the hot rice over the chicken, pressing the surface using wax paper.

- Let stand for 5 minutes, then turn the mold upside down on a warm platter, and serve.

Beans with Tuna and Scallions

Serves 4

2 cups cannelini beans (soak the beans overnight)
2 cloves garlic, mashed
¼ cup lemon juice
¼ cup olive oil
12 ounces tuna
2 cups scallions, chopped
salt and pepper to taste,
(use freshly ground black pepper)

- Mix garlic with the lemon juice, olive oil, the salt and freshly ground black pepper. Set on the side.
- In a heavy pot, boil the beans in salted water until they are soft, but not mushy. Remove from heat, drain, then add to the lemon olive oil dressing. Toss well.
- Add the tuna and mix gently.
- Sprinkle with the chopped scallions. Serve.

Cauliflower in Cilantro Tomato Sauce

Serves 4

1 pound cauliflower florets
4 tablespoons olive oil
1 small onion, chopped
4 cloves garlic, coarsely chopped
1 pound lean ground beef
1 32-ounce can diced tomatoes
2 cups fresh cilantro, chopped
1 cup garbanzo beans, cooked
salt and pepper to taste

- Place the cauliflower florets on a cookie sheet, spray with olive oil and broil until golden brown. Remove from the oven and set aside.
- Heat olive oil in a heavy pot, then cook the onions for a few minutes.
- Add the beef, stir and cook over medium heat for 10 minutes.
- Add the diced tomatoes, two cups of water, garlic, salt and pepper. Stir and bring to a boil.
- Drop in the cauliflower and garbanzo beans, then bring back to a boil. Cover and simmer for 10 minutes.
- Stir in the fresh cilantro and remove from heat. Serve with rice.

Stuffed Zucchini in Cilantro Sauce

Serves 4

- 1 pound lean ground beef
- 1 medium onion, chopped
- 4 large zucchini squash
- 4 tablespoons olive oil
- 2 tablespoons butter
- 2 cloves garlic, mashed
- 2 tablespoons soy flour
- 1 cup cilantro, chopped
- 2 cups skim milk
- ½ teaspoon black pepper
- ½ teaspoon white pepper
- ¼ teaspoon freshly ground nutmeg
- ½ cup Parmesan cheese
- salt to taste

• In a deep pot, bring salted water to a boil. Cut the zucchini lengthwise in half and drop zucchini in the boiling water. Bring back to a boil and boil for 5 minutes. Remove the zucchini from the water and, with a teaspoon, scoop out the insides of the zucchini. Place the zucchini halves, cut side up, on a greased baking pan.

To make the stuffing:

• Heat two tablespoons of olive oil in a pan, add half of the mashed garlic. Sauté for a few seconds. Add the ground beef, salt and pepper. Stir and cook until meat is done. Remove from the oven and set aside.

(Continued on next page)

To make the sauce:

- Heat the rest of the olive oil and the butter in a sauce pan, and cook the garlic for a few seconds. Add the cilantro and sauté for a couple of minutes. Remove from heat, add the flour and blend a little bit. Place the pot back on the heat. Add the milk gradually, whisking constantly to prevent lumps. Add the white pepper, nutmeg and salt. Cook over low heat until the sauce slightly thickens.

To assemble:

- Spoon the beef into the zucchini halves. Pour the sauce over the stuffed zucchini. Sprinkle the Parmesan cheese on top, then bake in a 375 degree oven for 30 minutes or until the cheese is golden. Serve.

Black Bean Tart

Serves 6

1½ cups sweet white sorghum flour
1 teaspoon ground cumin
½ teaspoon ground coriander
½ teaspoon paprika
½ teaspoon salt
4 tablespoons butter
1 cup sour cream
¼ cup fresh cilantro, chopped
1 cup black beans, cooked
1 cup whole kernel corn
1 cup scallions, chopped
½ cup red bell pepper, chopped
½ cup shredded cheddar cheese
salt to taste

- Mix flour, cumin, coriander, paprika and salt.
- Add the butter and a little water to form the dough.
- Press the dough onto the bottom and sides of a 10-inch tart pan with a removable, fluted rim. Bake in a 350 degree oven for 10 minutes. Remove from the oven and allow it to cool.
- In a food processor puree a half cup of the cooked black beans with one tablespoon of the chopped cilantro and the sour cream.
- Mix the rest of the ingredients, except for the cheddar cheese. Set aside.

(Continued on next page)

To assemble:

- Spread the bean sour cream sauce inside the baked shell. Spoon the bean vegetable mixture on top of the sour cream. Sprinkle with the cheddar cheese. Bake in a 350 degree oven for 10 minutes. Remove from the oven, cool on a rack for 10 minutes and serve.

Broiled Vegetable Pie

Serves 4-6

2 cups sweet white sorghum flour
½ cup rice flour
5 tablespoons butter
2 tablespoons olive oil
1 red bell pepper, thinly sliced
1 green bell pepper, thinly sliced
1 medium onion, julienne
1 cup ricotta cheese
½ cup feta cheese
1 teaspoon thyme
½ cup Kalamata olives, chopped
1 egg
1 tablespoon sesame seeds

- Toss the vegetables with the olive oil, place on a cookie sheet and broil until soft and slightly charred. Remove from the oven and cool.
- Mix the sorghum flour with the rice flour, the butter and cold water. Mix until you have smooth dough.
- Place the dough on a parchment paper, which has been placed on a cookie sheet, and roll into a ⅛-inch thick circle.
- Mix the ricotta cheese with the feta cheese, olives and thyme. Spoon this mixture on the dough and gently smooth to cover the circle, except for 1-inch for the edge.

(Continued on next page)

- Spoon the vegetables over the cheese, then fold about 1-inch of dough around the vegetables to form an edge.
- Whisk the egg and brush it onto the dough. Sprinkle with the sesame seeds and bake in a 375 degree oven until golden. Remove from the oven, cool for 10 minutes and serve.

Zucchini with Lima Beans and Kasha Pilaf

Serves 4-6

1 cup roasted Kasha*
¼ cup olive oil
1 medium onion, finely chopped
2 cups medium zucchini, finely chopped
2 cups frozen lima beans, thawed
2 cloves garlic, mashed
1 cup fresh cilantro, chopped
salt and pepper to taste

- Heat the olive oil and sauté the onions for a couple of minutes.
- Add the zucchini and 2½ cups of water, stir, cover and cook over medium heat for 10 minutes.
- Add the lima beans, kasha, garlic, cilantro and seasoning. Stir and cook for 15 minutes. Serve.

Kasha Lentil Pilaf

Serves 6

2 cups lentils
1 cup Kasha*
2 medium onion, julienne
¼ cup olive oil
salt to taste

- In a heavy saucepan, heat the olive oil, and then fry the onion until golden.
- Remove the onions from the oil and set aside.
- Add the lentils to the oil, the salt and three cups of water to a boil. When the lentils are done but not soft, add the kasha. Stir and bring back to a boil. Cover and cook over low heat for 10 minutes.
- Remove from the heat and allow the pilaf to rest for 10 minutes.
- Spoon the pilaf into a shallow serving platter, sprinkle with the golden onions and serve.

Beef Kibbeh

Serves 6-8

2 cups Kasha*
2 pounds ground lean beef
1 medium onion, cut into quarters
2 medium onions, finely chopped
6 tablespoons olive oil
2 tablespoons pine nuts (optional)
1 teaspoon allspice
½ teaspoon nutmeg
½ teaspoon cumin
½ teaspoon black pepper
salt to taste

To make Kibbeh stuffing:

- Heat four tablespoons of the olive oil in a frying pan. Add the chopped onions and cook for couple of minutes.
- Add half pound of the ground beef, half teaspoon allspice, the pine nuts and the salt. Stir and cook until the beef is cooked. Remove from the heat and allow to cool for few minutes.

To make the Kibbeh:

- Bring three cups of water to a boil. Add the kasha and cook for 5 minutes or until the kasha is soft. Remove from the heat. Drain and squeeze any excess water.

(Continued on next page)

- In a food processor, process the rest of the meat with the quartered onion, the cooked kasha and the rest of the seasoning. Process the mixture until well mixed and finely ground.
- Remove from the processor into a chilled bowl and mix thoroughly.

To assemble the Kibbeh:

- Divide the Kibbeh in half. Spread one portion on the bottom of a oiled baking dish.
- Spread the Kibbeh stuffing evenly over the first layer.
- Cut the second half of the Kibbeh into four balls, flatten each ball into ¼-inch thick round, and then place on top of the stuffing. Repeat the same steps with the rest of the balls. Cover and pat evenly the Kibbeh.
- Use the rest of the olive oil to smooth the surface.

- With a sharp knife, cut the Kibbeh into diamond shape.
- Bake in a 375 degree oven for 40 minutes or until golden brown.

Kasha with Tomato and Garbanzo Beans Pilaf

Serves 6

4 tablespoons olive oil
1 medium onion, finely chopped
1 16-ounce can diced tomatoes
1 cup garbanzo beans, cooked
1 cup Kasha*
salt and pepper to taste

- In a heavy saucepan, heat the olive oil and sauté the chopped onions for couple of minutes.
- Add the diced tomatoes, the garbanzo beans, one cup of water and seasoning. Bring to a boil.
- Add the kasha and bring back to a boil. Cover and cook over low heat for 10 minutes.
- Remove from the heat and allow the pilaf to rest for 10 minutes before serving.

Rice with Noodles

Serves 4

3 tablespoons olive oil
½ cup rice noodles, broken
1 cup basmati rice
salt to taste

- Heat the olive oil and brown the noodles in a frying pan.
- Add 2½ cups of water and a little salt. Bring to a boil.
- Add the rice, stir, cover and cook over very low heat for 20 minutes.
- Turn off the heat and allow rice to rest, covered, for 10 minutes. Serve.

Risotto with Eggplant and Cheese

Serves 6

1 large eggplant, cut into 1-inch cubes
4 tablespoons olive oil
1 clove garlic, diced
1 large ripe tomato, diced
1 medium onion, diced
1½ cups Arborio rice
5 cups gluten free chicken broth
(see recipe on page 175)
½ cup Parmesan cheese, grated
1 cup fresh mozzarella cheese, diced (optional)
¼ cup parsley, chopped
salt and pepper to taste

- Place the eggplant cubes on a cookie sheet, spray with olive oil and broil until golden. Remove and set aside.
- In a small pan, heat two tablespoons of olive oil and sauté the garlic for a few seconds. Add the diced tomato, salt and pepper, stir and cook over medium-low heat for a couple of minutes. Add the eggplant cubes, stir and cook over low heat for 5 minutes. Remove from heat and set aside.
- Place the broth in a pan, heat and allow it to simmer on low heat.
- In another pan, heat the rest of the olive oil and sauté the diced onion over low heat until soft. Add the rice, stir to make sure all the grain is well coated.

(Continued on next page)

- Add a half cup of the broth, stir and cook until well absorbed. Continue on adding a half cup of the broth at a time, stirring frequently to prevent sticking. Continue adding and stirring until rice is tender and soft.
- Add the tomato-eggplant mixture, the Parmesan cheese and the last half a cup of broth. Stir well until the cheese is melted and the broth is absorbed. Remove from heat. Sprinkle in the parsley and mozzarella cheese, stir gently and serve.

Eggplant Parmesan

Serves 4

1 large eggplant, cut into half-inch thick slices
1 egg
1 cup rice crackers, ground
2 tablespoons almond flour
¼ cup olive oil
4 ounces fresh mozzarella cheese
½ cup Parmesan cheese
1 cup tomato sauce (see recipe on page 122)

- Place the eggplant slices on a cookie sheet. Spray with olive oil spray and broil until golden. Turn over, spray again and broil until golden brown. Remove and set aside.
- Mix the ground rice crackers with the almond flour.
- Whisk the egg with one tablespoon water.
- Brush the eggplant slices with egg mixture, then slightly dip them in the flour mixture.
- Heat the olive oil and fry the eggplant slices until golden. Remove and set aside.
- In a small baking dish, place the eggplant slices on the bottom. Top with a slice of mozzarella for the first layer, then layer the tomato sauce. Sprinkle with the Parmesan cheese.
- Bake in a 375 degree oven for 15 minutes. Remove from the oven and serve.

Basic Tomato Sauce

Makes 2 cups

4 tablespoons olive oil
4 cloves garlic, mashed
1 16-ounce can tomato sauce with no sugar
2 tablespoons fresh basil, chopped
salt to taste

- Heat the olive oil and sauté the garlic for a few seconds.
- Add the rest of the ingredients. Stir and cook over medium heat for 10 minutes.

Rice and Eggplant with Tomato and Garbanzo Bean Pilaf

Serves 4

1 large eggplant, cut into 1-inch thick cubes
1 medium onion, chopped
3 tablespoons olive oil
1 16-ounce can diced tomatoes
1 cup garbanzo beans, cooked
1 cup short grain rice
salt and pepper to taste

- Place the eggplant cubes on a cookie sheet, spray with olive oil spray and broil until golden. Remove from the oven and set aside.
- Heat the olive oil and cook the onions for 5 minutes. Add the tomatoes, beans, salt and pepper. Stir and simmer for 5 minutes.
- Remove half of the tomato bean sauce and set aside.
- Spoon the broiled eggplant cubes into the tomato bean mixture inside the pot.
- Spread the rice over the eggplants, then pour the rest of the tomato-bean mixture and 1½ cups water. Bring to a boil, cover and cook over low heat for 25 minutes. Remove from heat and allow it to cool for 5 minutes before serving.

Rice with Carrots, Peas and Almonds

Serves 4

4 tablespoons almonds, slivered
¼ cup olive oil
2 cups frozen peas, thawed
1 cup carrots, diced
1 cup basmati rice
salt and pepper to taste

- Heat the olive oil and cook the almonds until golden.
- Add 2¼ cups of water, peas, carrots, salt and pepper. Bring to a boil.
- Add the rice, stir and bring back to a boil. Cover and cook over low heat for 25 minutes. Serve hot.

Rice with Vegetables, Raisins and Ginger

Serves 4

¼ cup olive oil
½ cup almonds, slivered
1 small onion, finely chopped
1 clove garlic, mashed
1 green bell pepper, finely diced
1 red bell pepper, finely diced
1 large tomato, diced
1 cup raisins
½ teaspoon ginger
½ teaspoon nutmeg
1 cup basmati rice
4 scallions, chopped
salt and pepper to taste

- Heat the olive oil in a heavy pot, then cook the almonds until golden. Remove the almonds from the pot and set aside.
- Add the onions and garlic to the oil and cook over medium-low heat for 10 minutes.
- Add the rest of the vegetables, except for the scallions. Stir and cook for a couple of minutes.
- Add 2¼ cups of water, the raisins, ginger, nutmeg, salt and pepper. Bring to a boil.
- Add the rice, stir, then bring back to a boil.
- Cover and cook over very low heat for 25 minutes. Remove from heat. Allow the rice to rest, then spoon it into a shallow serving platter. Sprinkle the scallions and almonds on top of the rice before serving.

Layered Mushroom Potato Bake

Serves 6-8

5 potatoes, boiled
½ cup Parmesan cheese
1 clove garlic, mashed
½ cup sour cream
3 tablespoons olive oil
½ pound ground beef
2 medium onions, chopped
1 pound mushrooms, sliced
½ cup cilantro, chopped
3 tablespoons Pomegranate Molasses*
½ cup walnuts, chopped and toasted (optional)
salt and pepper to taste

- Peel and mash the potatoes. Mix in the garlic, Parmesan cheese, sour cream, salt and pepper.
- In a frying pan, heat the olive oil and cook the onions until golden. Add the ground beef and a little salt, stir and cook over medium heat until the beef is thoroughly cooked. Add the mushrooms, stir and cook for a few minutes. Add the pomegranate molasses and cilantro. Stir and remove from heat.
- Spoon the beef and mushroom mixture into a baking dish. Gently spread the mashed potatoes over the beef mixture. Bake in a 375 degree oven for 25 minutes or until the top of the potatoes are golden. Remove from the oven, sprinkle with the chopped walnuts and serve.

Stuffed Potatoes

Serves 4

8 medium potatoes
4 tablespoons olive oil
1 small onion, chopped
½ pound lean ground beef
1 teaspoon allspice
1 16-ounce can diced tomatoes
1 tablespoon tomato paste
2 cups water
1 clove garlic, mashed
½ teaspoon basil
salt and pepper to taste

- Peel the potatoes, then hollow a pocket in them, leaving a half-inch thick wall, which you should try not to pierce. To prevent a change of color, place the potatoes in cold water until you are ready to use them.
- Heat the olive oil in a frying pan and cook the onions for a few minutes. Add the beef, allspice, salt and pepper and cook until beef is cooked through.
- Stuff the potatoes with the beef stuffing, then arrange the stuffed potatoes in a shallow baking tray.
- Mix diced tomatoes, tomato paste, water, garlic, basil and salt. Pour this mixture over the stuffed potatoes.
- Bake in a 375 degree oven for 45 minutes. Remove from the oven and serve.

Thin Beef Steak with Mushrooms in Lemon Garlic Sauce

Serves 4

1 pound steak, thinly sliced
   (top sirloin is preferred)
1 teaspoon allspice
4 tablespoons olive oil
8 cloves garlic, mashed
½ cup lemon juice
1 16-ounce can of whole mushrooms
1 cup fresh or frozen sweet peas
   salt and pepper to taste

- Rub the beef slices with the allspice.
- Heat the olive oil and sear the steaks on both sides. Remove the beef and set aside.
- Add the garlic to the frying pan, stir for 1 minute, then pour in the lemon juice, ¼ cup water, salt and pepper. Bring to a boil.
- Add the mushrooms with the juice and the peas. Bring back to a boil.
- Add the seared thin steaks, cover and simmer for 10 minutes. Serve with mashed potatoes.

Beef Rolls with Lima Beans

Serves 4

1 pound lean beef, thinly sliced (top sirloin is preferred)
8 ounces provolone cheese, remove any rind
1 clove garlic, mashed
8 basil leaves, chopped
½ cup rice flour
6 tablespoons olive oil
1 tablespoon butter
4 sage leaves, chopped
1 teaspoon thyme
1 medium onion, thinly sliced
1 cup red wine
2 cups gluten free beef broth (see recipe on page 174)
1 28-ounce can diced tomatoes
1 pound frozen lima beans, thawed
salt and pepper to taste

- Chop the cheese and mix with the garlic, half of the basil and a little salt.
- Lay the beef slices on a plate, scoop about one tablespoon of the cheese mixture onto the beef. Roll up the beef and tie the beef rolls with kitchen twine. Coat the beef rolls in the flour.
- Heat the olive oil and brown the beef rolls lightly on both sides. Set aside.

(Continued on next page)

- Add butter to the pan and cook the sage and basil in the butter-oil mixture for a few seconds. Add the thinly sliced onions, wine, and the beef broth. Cover and cook over low heat for 10 minutes.
- Add the diced tomatoes and seasoning, stir and bring to a boil. Place the beef rolls in the pan, cover and cook over medium heat for 1 hour.
- Add the lima beans and a little of the boiling water if the sauce begins thickening. Continue cooking for another half an hour.
- Remove from the heat, remove the twine and serve with plain rice.

Braised Veal Shanks with Parsley Pesto

Serves 4

8 2-inch thick pieces of veal shank
½ cup rice flour
2 tablespoons butter
4 tablespoons olive oil
1 medium onion, finely chopped
1 celery stalk, finely chopped
1 medium carrot, finely chopped
1 cup dry white wine
1 16-ounce can diced tomatoes
½ teaspoon thyme
1 clove garlic, mashed
¼ teaspoon basil
2 cups beef broth
½ cup parsley
2 cloves garlic
2 tablespoons olive oil
¼ cup walnuts
salt and pepper to taste

- In a large casserole (the casserole should be large enough to hold the veal in one layer) heat two tablespoons of olive oil, then sauté the onions for a couple of minutes. Add the carrots and celery. Stir and cook until the vegetables are softened. Set aside.
- Lightly dust the veal shank with the rice flour. Heat the rest of the oil and the butter in a frying pan, until butter begins to foam. Place the floured shanks in the pan. Turn the shanks until they are browned on all

(Continued on next page)

sides. Remove from the frying pan and place over the cooked vegetables in the casserole.

- Pour the wine in the frying pan. Boil for 2 minutes while scraping the sides and bottom of the pan, then pour the juice over the veal shanks in the casserole.
- Mix the tomatoes with the broth, garlic, thyme, basil, salt and pepper. Pour over the veal shanks. Place the casserole back on the heat and bring it to a boil. Remove from heat, cover and bake in a 350 degree oven for 2 to 3 hours.

To make parsley pesto:

- In a food processor, puree parsley, garlic, walnuts, oil and salt until you have a smooth paste.

To serve:

- Place two shanks on a plate. Spoon some of the sauce over and around the veal. Top each veal shank with a teaspoon of the parsley pesto and serve.

Chicken Shish Tawook

Serves 4

4 chicken breasts, cut into 1-inch cubes
4 tablespoons olive oil
2 cloves garlic, mashed
1 tablespoon mustard
½ teaspoon ground cumin
2 tablespoons vinegar
1 tablespoon tomato paste
3 tablespoons honey
½ cup water
salt to taste

- Heat olive oil in a small pan. Add the garlic and cook for a few seconds. Add the vinegar and move from heat. Add the rest of the ingredients, except for the chicken breasts. Stir and cook for a couple of minutes.
- Skewer the chicken breast cubes on eight skewers. Rub the chicken pieces with the garlic marinade, cover and refrigerate for a couple of hours.
- Broil or grill until golden and chicken is done. Serve hot.

Chicken in Garlic Lemon Sauce

Serves 4

4 chicken breasts
2 large potatoes
3 tablespoons olive oil
6 cloves garlic, mashed
½ cup lemon juice
½ cup water
1 teaspoon paprika
1 teaspoon thyme
zest of one lemon
salt to taste

- Boil the potatoes for 5 minutes. Remove from the water and slice into half-inch thick slices.
- Mix the olive oil, garlic, lemon juice, lemon zest, paprika, thyme and salt. Rub the chicken pieces in the olive oil-garlic mixture, and place them in a baking dish.
- Fit the potatoes between the chicken pieces. Pour what is left of the sauce on top of the chicken. Cover the baking dish with foil and bake at 375 degrees for 30 minutes.
- Remove the foil and continue to bake for another 15 minutes or until the chicken pieces are golden. Serve.

Fish in Tahini Sauce

Serves 4-6

2 pounds white fish
½ teaspoon black pepper
4 tablespoons olive oil
1 cup lemon juice
¼ cup Tahini*
6 cloves garlic, mashed
1 teaspoon ground cumin
½ cup parsley, chopped
salt to taste

- Mix the black pepper with ¼ cup lemon juice and the olive oil. Rub the fish inside and out with this mixture.
- Bake uncovered in an oiled pan at 400 degrees for about 20-30 minutes until the fish is flaky.
- Whisk the rest of the lemon juice with the rest of the garlic, Tahini, cumin, water and salt. Add a little more water if the sauce is somewhat thick. Add the parsley and mix well.
- Remove the fish from the oven, pour the Tahini-parsley sauce over the fish and serve.

Canned Tuna with Spicy Walnut Sauce

Serves 4

14 ounces canned tuna (or tuna sold in a sealed aluminum packet, which will do quite well)
4 cloves garlic, mashed
4 tablespoons olive oil
1 small onion, finely chopped
1 red bell pepper, finely chopped
½ cup walnuts, finely chopped and toasted
1 teaspoon cayenne pepper
1 teaspoon ground cumin
1 teaspoon ground coriander
¼ cup lemon juice
salt to taste

- Heat the olive oil in a heavy pan; add the onions and sauté for 5 minutes or until soft.
- Add the red bell pepper, garlic and walnuts, allow to cook for a couple of minutes while stirring.
- Add the cayenne pepper, cumin, coriander, salt and lemon juice. Stir and cook for 2 minutes.
- Add the tuna, stir and cook for a couple of minutes. Serve.

Spiced Salmon Steak

Serves 4

4 6-ounce salmon steaks, 1-inch thick
½ cup olive oil
1 teaspoon coriander seeds
1 teaspoon cumin seeds
1 teaspoon red pepper, crushed
salt to taste

- Toast coriander and cumin seeds over medium heat in a cast-iron skillet for about 3 minutes, while shaking the skillet. Remove and cool for a few minutes.
- Grind the toasted seeds and the crushed pepper into a powder.
- Rub each steak with the spicy powder.
- In a large non-stick skillet, heat the olive oil and cook each steak until browned on both sides. Serve.

Fish and Rice Pilaf

Serves 4

1 cup olive oil
1 pound fish fillet, cut into 2-inch pieces
1 teaspoon cumin
2 medium onions, julienne
1 cup rice
½ cup pine nuts, toasted until golden
salt and pepper to taste

- Heat the olive oil and cook the fish pieces until golden. Remove the fish and set aside.
- In the same pot, cook the onions until golden brown.
- Add 2¼ cups of water to the onions and bring to a boil.
- Add the rice, cumin and salt. Stir and bring back to a boil. Drop in the fish pieces, cover and cook over very low heat for 20 minutes. Remove from heat and allow the rice to rest for 5 minutes before serving.

To serve:

- Scoop the rice pilaf into a serving bowl, sprinkle with the pine nuts, and serve.

Fish Stew

Serves 4

½ cup olive oil
1 pound shrimp, shelled, de-veined, and cooked
1 pound filled, fillet and cut into 2-inch pieces
1 medium onion, chopped
4 cloves garlic, mashed
½ teaspoon cumin
½ teaspoon coriander
½ teaspoon ginger
½ teaspoon cayenne pepper or red pepper paste
1 19-ounce can diced tomatoes
2 medium potatoes, cut into 1-inch cubes
½ cup fresh cilantro, chopped
salt to taste

- In a saucepan, heat the one-fourth cup olive oil and sauté the shrimp until golden. Remove and set aside. Add the rest of the olive oil and heat. Sauté the fish until golden. Remove and set the fish aside.
- In the same pan, cook the onion until soft. Add the garlic and all of the seasoning. Stir and cook for 1 minute.
- Add the diced tomatoes and the potatoes, stir and bring to a boil. Cover and simmer over medium heat until the potatoes are soft, about 15 minutes.
- Add the shrimp, fish, and cilantro, stir gently and continue cooking for another 5 minutes or until shrimp is thoroughly cooked. Serve.

Chicken Breast with Pepper and Pearl Onions

Serves 4

4 chicken breasts
4 tablespoons olive oil
2 tablespoons butter
1 red bell pepper, julienne
1 pound frozen pearl onions, thawed
1 clove garlic, mashed
½ teaspoon fresh ginger, grated
⅛ teaspoon nutmeg
1 tablespoon corn starch
salt to taste

- Heat the olive oil and sear the chicken breasts until golden. Remove from the pan and set aside.
- Add the pepper and pearl onions to the same pan, stir and sauté for 5 minutes. Remove the vegetables from the pan and set aside.
- Add the butter, heat and sauté the garlic and the ginger for 1 minute.
- Add the chicken back into the pot. Pour three cups of water over the chicken breasts. Bring to a boil, cover and simmer for 10 minutes. Add the vegetables and stir.
- Mix cornstarch with one cup of water, nutmeg and salt. Pour over the chicken, stir. Continue cooking for 5 minutes, stirring often. Remove the pot from heat and allow it to cool for 5 minutes and serve.

Chicken with Garbanzo Beans and Almonds

Serves 4-6

- 8 chicken thighs
- ¼ cup olive oil
- 2 medium onions, coarsely chopped
- 4 cloves garlic, mashed
- ½ cup cilantro, chopped
- ½ teaspoon coriander
- ½ teaspoon cinnamon
- 2 cups garbanzo beans, cooked
- 2 tablespoons honey
- ½ cup almonds, slivered and toasted
- salt and pepper to taste

- Heat the olive oil and sear the chicken until golden on both sides.
- Add the onion, garlic, cilantro, coriander, salt and pepper. Stir and sauté for a couple of minutes.
- Add four cups of water and bring to a boil. Cover and cook over medium heat for 1 hour or until chicken is done. Remove the chicken pieces from the pot and set aside.
- Add the honey, almonds, cinnamon and garbanzo beans. Place the chicken on top of the sauce, cover and continue simmering until the sauce is thickened. Serve.

Pesto Pasta Mold

Serves 6

12 ounces lite tofu, drained
6 cloves garlic
½ cup plus 2 tablespoons of Parmesan cheese, grated
½ cup basil, chopped
¼ cup olive oil
1 pound store-bought gluten-free spaghetti
salt to taste

- In a food processor, puree tofu, garlic, half cup Parmesan cheese, basil, olive oil and salt into a smooth paste.
- In a large pot, bring salted water to a boil. Add the pasta and cook until al-dente. Drain the pasta, then mix well until all pasta is coated with the basil tofu paste.
- Spray a bundt cake pan with olive oil, then sprinkle with two tablespoons of Parmesan cheese.
- Stuff the cake pan with the pasta. Press the pasta very firmly into the cake pan.
- Bake in a 375 degree oven for 35 minutes.
- Place a flat serving platter on top of the cake pan. Quickly invert the pan upside down. Leave the pan on top for a couple of minutes, then remove the pan. Cut and serve.

Lentils with Mushrooms and Kale Lasagna

Serves 6

6 sheets gluten-free Lasagna
½ pound lentils
4 tablespoons olive oil
1 medium onion, julienne
2 cloves garlic, mashed
1 pound white mushrooms, sliced
2 cups kale, chopped
1 cup cilantro, chopped
2 tablespoons tomato paste
¼ cup Pomegranate Molasses*
1 cup tomato sauce (see recipe on page 122)
½ cup mozzarella cheese, grated
salt and pepper to taste

- Boil the lentils until they are done, but not soft. Drain and set aside.
- Bring water to a boil. Drop in the kale, bring back to a boil and allow the kale to cook for a couple of minutes. Remove from heat, drain and cool, then squeeze excess water.
- In a pan, heat the olive oil and cook the onions until golden. Add the garlic and mushrooms. Stir and cook until soft. Add half cup of water, the tomato paste, pomegranate molasses, salt and pepper.
- Add the lentils, cilantro and kale. Stir and set aside.

(Continued on next page)

- Bring salted water to a boil. Drop the lasagna sheets in the water and cook until al-dente.
- Place half of the lasagna sheets in a baking tray. Spoon the lentil and kale mixture on top of the lasagna sheets. Place the rest of the lasagna sheets on top. Spread on the tomato sauce, then sprinkle with the cheese.
- Bake in a 400 degree oven for 25 minutes. Serve.

Spinach Gnocchi in Tomato Sauce

Serves 4

- 1 pound gluten free ricotta cheese (see recipe on page 172)
- 10 ounces frozen spinach, thawed and chopped
- 2 eggs
- 1 cup soy flour
- ½ cup Parmesan cheese
- ¼ teaspoon nutmeg
- ¼ teaspoon black pepper
- 2 cups tomato sauce (see recipe on page 122)
- zest of one lemon
- salt to taste

- Spoon the ricotta cheese onto a cheesecloth and drain well.
- Squeeze excess water from the spinach, then place the spinach in a mixing bowl.
- Add the ricotta cheese, eggs, Parmesan cheese, half cup of the flour, lemon zest and the seasoning. Mix well.
- Make 1-inch balls from the spinach mixture and dip them in the rest of the flour, making sure they are well coated with the flour. Use more flour if needed.
- In a heavy pot, bring three quarts of water to a boil. Drop gnocchi into the boiling water, four or five at a time. Boil for 2 minutes. Remove spinach gnocchi from the water and place in a 8x14 inch baking pan.
- Cover with the tomato sauce, then bake in a 375 degree oven for 30 minutes. Remove from the oven and serve.

Spinach Tortellini

Serves 4

1 pound frozen spinach, thawed
½ cup gluten free ricotta cheese
(see recipe on page 172)
1 clove garlic, mashed
1 basic pasta dough (see recipe on page 158)
4 tablespoons olive oil
4 scallions, chopped
4 medium tomatoes, diced
¼ cup fresh basil, chopped
2 tablespoons fresh Parmesan cheese, grated
zest of one lemon
dash of nutmeg
salt to taste

- Squeeze excess water from the spinach. Add the cheese, garlic, lemon zest, nutmeg and salt.
- Roll the dough into ⅛-inch thick slices, then cut into 2-inch squares. Put a teaspoon of the spinach mixture onto each square.
- Fold the tortellini into a triangle, and, using a fork, press the edges to seal.
- Bring salted water to a boil. Drop in the tortellini and cook until just al-dente. Drain.
- Meanwhile, heat the olive oil, then add the scallions and diced tomatoes. Stir and add the tortellini, basil and salt. Cook together for few minutes. Serve.

Tortellini with Spinach and Cheese

Serves 4

1 pasta dough, either soy or sorghum
8 ounces frozen chopped spinach leaves, thawed
1 cup gluten free ricotta cheese
(see recipe on page 172)
4 tablespoons Parmesan cheese
4 tablespoons olive oil
2 cloves garlic, mashed
4 medium ripe tomatoes, finely diced
2 tablespoons tomato paste
2 tablespoons fresh basil, chopped
zest of one lemon
salt and pepper to taste

To make the stuffing:

- Squeeze the water from the thawed spinach. Add cheeses, lemon zest and salt. Set aside.

- Remove the plastic wrap from the pasta dough and cut into four parts. Take one part and cover the other three parts.
- Dust a clean surface with a little flour and roll the dough into a disk. With a rolling pin, roll the dough from the center and away from you. Dust with a little flour, turn and repeat. Keep rolling and turning the dough until you have a flat and thin dough. The dough should be as thin as 1/8 -inch thick. Repeat with the rest of the parts of the dough. Cover the pasta sheets with a kitchen towel to prevent drying.

(Continued on next page)

- Cut the pasta sheets into 2-inch squares. Put about one teaspoon of the spinach stuffing onto each square. Moisten the edge of each square with a little of water, then fold the tortellini into triangles and firmly seal the edges with your fingertips. Set aside.
- In a large pasta pan, bring salted water to a boil. Drop in the tortellini and cook for 5 minutes. Remove and drain when the tortellini are al-dente.
- Meanwhile, heat the olive oil and cook the garlic for a few seconds. Add the diced tomatoes, tomato paste, fresh basil and seasoning. Stir and cook for a couple of minutes. Add about a half cup of water if the sauce is a little thick.
- Add the cooked tortellini to the tomato sauce and cook together for a couple of minutes.

Polenta with Mushroom Sauce

Serves 4-6

1 cup milk
1 tablespoon butter
2 cups corn meal
4 tablespoons olive oil
1 small onion, chopped
1 pound white mushrooms, thinly sliced
1 clove garlic, mashed
1 cup gluten free vegetable broth (see recipe on page 173)
½ teaspoon thyme
½ teaspoon ginger
¼ teaspoon nutmeg
1 cup milk
¼ cup heavy cream
2 tablespoons cornstarch

- Bring to a boil, one cup of milk, four cups of water, the butter and a little salt. Add the corn meal gradually. Cook the polenta for 30 minutes, stirring often.
- Heat olive oil in a separate pan and sauté the onion until soft. Add the garlic and mushrooms. Stir and cook for 5 minutes.
- Add the vegetable broth and the thyme, nutmeg, and ginger. Stir and cook for a couple of minutes.
- Mix the cornstarch with the milk and the heavy cream, then pour over the cooked mushrooms.

(Continued on next page)

Simmer over medium heat until the sauce thickens, stirring frequently.

- Scoop the polenta onto a flat serving dish and pour the mushroom sauce on top. Serve.

Moroccan Couscous

Serves 4-6

3 cups quinoa
½ cup olive oil
1 cup medium onion, chopped
1 pound chicken pieces
1 pound stew beef
2 tablespoons tomato paste
1 28-ounce can crushed tomatoes
½ pound baby carrots
1 zucchini, cut into 1-inch thick pieces
1 acorn squash, seeded and cut into 1-inch thick pieces
1 16-ounce can garbanzo beans, drained
½ teaspoon cumin
½ teaspoon coriander
1 jalapeno pepper, pierce with a fork several times
salt to taste

To make the couscous:

- Heat two tablespoons of olive oil, add the quinoa , stir, then add four cups of boiling water and butter. Stir and bring back to a boil. Cook for 5 minutes. Remove from heat. Set aside.
- To make the stew: In a deep pot, heat the rest of the olive oil and cook the onions until transparent. Add the beef, chicken and one cup of water. Cover and simmer for 10 minutes.

(Continued on next page)

- Pour in eight cups of water, the tomato paste, crushed tomatoes, jalapeno and the rest of the seasoning. Bring to a boil, cover and allow it to simmer for 30 minutes.
- Add the vegetables and bring back to a boil, simmer until vegetables are tender. Adjust the seasoning, then add the garbanzo beans. Cook for 5 minutes.

To serve:

- Squeeze any excess water from the quinoa, then mix with one cup of the sauce from the stew, toss and scoop into a shallow serving platter. Arrange the meat and vegetables on top of the quinoa couscous. Pour the rest of the stew into a bowl and serve with the couscous.

Three Sauce Lasagna

Serves 4

28 fresh corn tortillas, cut into 3-inch squares
2 cups basic tomato sauce (see recipe on page 122)
2 cups basil pesto sauce (see recipe on page 154)
2 cups white sauce (see recipe on page 155)
½ cup Parmesan cheese

- Spread half cup of the tomato sauce on the bottom of an 8x12 pan.
- Cover the sauce with six corn tortillas.
- Spread half of the pesto sauce over the corn sheet.
- Cover the pesto with corn tortillas.
- Spread half of the white sauce over the pasta sheet.
- Repeat until you finish with the tomato sauce on top
- Sprinkle with Parmesan cheese and bake in a 375 degree oven for 15 minutes. Remove and serve.

Basil Pesto Sauce

Makes 2 cups

2 cups fresh basil, chopped
6 cloves garlic
½ cup olive oil
½ cup Parmesan cheese
zest of one lemon
salt to taste

- Place the ingredients in a food processor and puree the mixture until a smooth paste.

White Sauce

Makes 3 cups

- 4 tablespoons olive oil
- 3 tablespoons white sorghum flour
- 3 cups milk
- ¼ teaspoon nutmeg
- ¼ teaspoon white pepper
- salt to taste

- Heat the olive oil in a saucepan and blend in the flour.
- Add the milk and the rest of the ingredients. Whisk and cook, stirring often, over medium heat until the sauce slightly thickens.

Spanish Paella

Serves 4

½ cup olive oil
2 pounds chicken pieces
½ pound fresh green beans,
  cut into 2-inch long pieces
1 teaspoon paprika
2 medium tomatoes, finely diced
4 cups gluten free chicken broth
  (see recipe on page 175)
1 tablespoon rosemary
2½ cups medium-grain rice
Pinch of saffron (optional)
salt to taste

- Heat the olive oil in a paella pan (shallow metal pan) and fry the chicken pieces until golden.
- Add the green beans and fry gently.
- Add the tomato, paprika, salt and the chicken broth. Bring quickly to a boil, then turn down the heat and cook on low heat for 30 minutes or until the meat is done.
- Add the rosemary and saffron. Stir and bring back to a boil. Add the rice and spread it as evenly as possible. Cook on high heat for the first 10 minutes. Turn down the heat and cook for another 10 minutes. Remove from heat and allow the paella to rest for 5 minutes before serving. The rice should be soft but firm. Serve.

Seafood Paella

Serves 6

¼ cup olive oil
2 cloves garlic, mashed
1 pound fish fillet, cut into 4 pieces
4 ounces shelled mussels
½ pound shelled shrimp
1 medium onion, finely chopped
1 red bell pepper, broiled, skin removed, seeded and chopped
2 cups rice
3 cups gluten free vegetable broth (see recipe on page 173)
1 teaspoon Spanish paprika
salt and pepper to taste

- Heat the olive oil in a large skillet and fry the garlic for a few seconds. Sear the fish pieces until cooked. Remove and set aside.
- In the same oil, fry the mussels, then set them aside.
- Fry the shrimp and set aside.
- Add the onion and fry until softened. Add the rice, red pepper, fish, shrimp and mussels. Stir gently.
- Add the broth, paprika, salt and black pepper. Stir and cook on medium-high for 10 minutes. Turn down the heat and simmer for another 10 minutes. Serve.

Soy Flour Pasta Dough (1)

Makes 2 cups

2½ cups soy flour
3 eggs
1 teaspoon salt
1 teaspoon olive oil

- Place the flour on a dry work surface.
- Make a large and deep well in the center of the flour.
- Crack the eggs into the well, then add the salt and olive oil. Mix the eggs with the salt and oil gently with a fork.
- Gradually start incorporating the flour from the sides of the well. Try not to break the sides of the well. Keep on incorporating and mixing the flour with the egg mixture until you have rough and sticky dough.
- Scrape up any dough from the work surface and from your fingers. Add a little cold water if the dough is a little dry or add a little flour if the dough too sticky to work with.
- Knead and fold the dough for 5-8 minutes. Press and push the dough away from you using the heel of your hand. Fold the end of the dough back on itself. Continue pressing and folding the dough until you have a very smooth and elastic dough.
- Wrap the dough in a plastic wrap and allow it to rest for 15 minutes at room temperature. The dough is now ready to be used to make any kind of pasta.

Sorghum Flour Pasta Dough (2)

Makes 2 cups

2½ cups sweet white sorghum flour
3 eggs
1 teaspoon salt
1 teaspoon olive oil

- Follow the same instructions as in the Soy Flour Pasta Dough (1) recipe on page 158.

Pasta with Chicken, Broccoli and Cream Sauce

Serves 4

- 2 cups small broccoli florets
- 2 chicken breasts, cooked and cut into thin strips
- 4 tablespoons olive oil
- 3 cloves garlic
- 1 cup milk
- 1 cup heavy cream
- ½ cup Gorgonzola cheese, crumbled
- ¼ cup Parmesan cheese
- 1 teaspoon rosemary, chopped
- 2 cups gluten-free short pasta
- salt and pepper to taste

- Bring salted water to a boil, drop the broccoli into the boiling water. Bring back to a boil. Cook for few minutes. Drain, rinse with cold water and set aside.
- Bring salted water to a boil, drop in the pasta and cook for 7 minutes or until al-dente.
- While the pasta is being cooked, warm the olive oil and cook the garlic for a few seconds. Add the milk, cream and seasoning.
- Add the chicken, stir, cover and cook over medium-low heat for 5 minutes.
- Add the Gorgonzola cheese and Parmesan cheese. Stir and cook over low heat for a couple of minutes.
- Add the broccoli and toss gently. Cook for a couple of minutes.
- Drain the pasta and add to the chicken sauce. Toss well.

Lamb Tajeen with Plum and Honey

Serves 4-6

¼ cup olive oil
2 pounds lamb, cut into 1-inch cubes
1 medium onion, finely chopped
1 cup cilantro, chopped
2 cloves garlic, mashed
1 teaspoon fresh ginger, chopped
½ teaspoon nutmeg
½ teaspoon coriander
½ teaspoon cardamom
1 pound plums
½ cup honey
½ cup sesame seeds
salt and pepper to taste

- Heat the olive oil and sauté the lamb cubes in a pan for 5 minutes.
- Add the onion, garlic, cilantro, ginger, nutmeg, coriander, cardamom and salt. Stir and cook for a couple of minutes.
- Add four cups of water, stir and bring to a boil. Cover and simmer for 1 hour.
- Add the honey and plums, stir and continue to cook for 10 minutes. Stir often.
- Spoon into a deep pot, sprinkle with the sesame seeds and serve.

Basic Savory Pie Dough

Makes 1 crust

1 cup Arborio rice
1 cup quinoa flakes
1 cup sweet white sorghum flour
2 tablespoons olive oil
½ teaspoon salt
½ teaspoon pepper

- Place the rice and six cups of water in a heavy soup pan. Bring to a boil. Turn the heat to medium and continue cooking, stirring often, until the water is almost gone and the rice is very sticky.
- Spoon the rice into a bowl and mashed it with a spoon. Add the rest of the ingredients and mix well until you have a little sticky dough. Wrap in plastic until ready to use.

Spinach and Walnut Pie

Serves 8

1 basic savory pie dough (see recipe on page 162)
8 ounces frozen spinach, thawed
4 tablespoons olive oil
1 medium onion, chopped
½ cup ricotta cheese
½ cup walnuts, chopped and toasted
zest of one lemon
salt and pepper to taste

- Heat two tablespoons of the olive oil in a pan. Sauté the onions in the olive oil until golden.
- Squeeze excess water from the spinach and add to the onion. Cook for a couple of minutes and remove from heat. Mix in the ricotta cheese, walnuts, lemon zest and seasoning.
- Grease a 10-inch pie plate with olive oil. Cut the dough into two balls.
- Press one ball into the greased pan. Cover the bottom and the sides.
- Spoon and spread the spinach mixture into the pie crust.
- Grease wax paper with olive oil. Place the second ball on the wax paper. Moisten your palm with olive oil and gently press the dough into a flat circle, then place another sheet of wax paper on top of the dough. Gently roll the dough into a 10-inch circle.

(Continued on next page)

Remove the top wax paper and flip the dough on top of the pie plate. Make a small hole in the center of the top crust as a steam vent. Seal and crimp the edges of the pie.

- Bake in a 400 degree oven for 45 minutes or until crust is golden brown. Remove from the oven. Cool slightly before serving.

Beef with Pomegranate Molasses Pie

Serves 8

1 basic savory pie dough (see recipe on page 162)
4 tablespoons olive oil
1 pound ground beef
1 large onion, chopped
6 ounces canned sliced mushrooms, drained
1 teaspoon ground cumin
2 cloves garlic, mashed
¼ cup Pomegranate Molasses*
½ teaspoon ground coriander
¼ teaspoon chili pepper
salt to taste

- Heat the olive oil, and sauté the onion for a couple of minutes. Add the beef, stir and cook over medium heat until it is cooked through. Add the rest of the ingredients and stir well. Drain any excess fat. Set the beef stuffing on the side.
- Grease a 10-inch pie plate with olive oil. Cut the dough into two balls.
- Press one ball into the greased pan. Cover the bottom and the sides.
- Spoon and spread the beef mixture into the pie crust.
- Grease wax paper with olive oil. Place the second dough ball on the wax paper. Moisten your palm with olive oil and gently press the dough into a flat circle, then place another sheet of wax paper on top of the dough. Gently roll the dough into a 10-inch circle. Remove the top wax paper and flip the

(Continued on next page)

dough on top of the pie plate. Make a small hole in the center of the top crust as a steam vent. Seal and crimp the edges of the pie.

- Bake in a 400 degree oven for 45 minutes or until crust is golden brown. Remove from the oven. Cool slightly before serving.

Cheese and Onions Pie

Serves 8

1 basic savory pie dough (see recipe on page 162)
1 cup feta cheese, crumbled
1 cup fresh Mozzarella cheese, chopped
¼ cup shredded Colby cheese
4 scallions, finely chopped
½ cup parsley, finely chopped
¼ teaspoon cayenne pepper
salt and pepper to taste

- Mix all stuffing ingredients together.
- Grease 10-inch pie plate with olive oil. Cut the dough into two balls.
- Press one ball into the greased pan. Cover the bottom and the sides.
- Spoon and spread the cheese mixture into the pie crust.
- Grease wax paper with olive oil. Place the second dough ball on the wax paper. Moisten your palm with olive oil and gently press the dough into a flat circle, then place another sheet of wax paper on top of the dough. Gently roll the dough into a 10-inch circle. Remove the top wax paper and flip the dough on top of the pie plate. Make a small hole in the center of the top crust as a steam vent. Seal and crimp the edges of the pie.
- Bake in a 400 degree oven for 45 minutes or until crust is golden brown. Remove from the oven. Cool slightly before serving.

Zucchini and Garbanzo Bean Stew

Serves 4

5 tablespoons olive oil
1 medium onion, chopped
4 cloves garlic, slivered
1 pound stew beef cubes
1 16-ounce can diced tomatoes
1 tablespoon tomato paste
2 zucchinis, cut into 1-inch cubes
2 cups garbanzo beans, cooked
½ teaspoon mint
½ teaspoon allspice
salt and pepper to taste

- Heat olive oil and sauté the onions until golden. Add garlic and beef. Stir and cook for 20 minutes or until beef is done.
- Add in the diced tomatoes, tomato paste, mint, allspice, salt and pepper. Bring to a boil, then simmer over low heat for 10 minutes.
- Add the zucchinis, stir, cover and continue to simmer for 20 minutes.
- Add the beans and cook for another 10 minutes, or until the zucchini is cooked and the liquid is mostly absorbed. Serve.

Cauliflower Quiche

Serves 6

1 cup rice flour
1½ cups white sweet sorghum flour
4 tablespoons butter
2 cups skim milk
½ teaspoon paprika
1 pound cauliflower
4 scallions, finely chopped
½ cup Swiss cheese, grated
½ cup Parmesan cheese, grated
2 eggs
a pinch of fresh ground nutmeg
salt and pepper to taste

- Mix one cup rice with one cup sorghum flour, a little salt and the paprika. Add the butter and half cup of milk. Mix, then add a little water to form a smooth ball.
- Spread the dough evenly in a 9-inch pie or quiche pan. Trim the edges. Bake in a 375 degree oven for 10 minutes. Remove from the oven.
- Cut the cauliflower into small florets, place on a cookie sheet and spray with olive oil spray. Broil until golden. Remove from the oven and set aside. Allow to cool. Arrange the florets on the bottom of the crust. Sprinkle the chopped scallion on top of the florets. Spread the Swiss cheese on top of the scallions.

(Continued on next page)

- Melt the butter and stir in the rest of the sorghum flour. Add the rest of the milk, nutmeg and a little salt. Whisk gently until slightly thickened. Remove from heat and stir in the eggs and Parmesan cheese. Pour this sauce on top of the vegetables.
- Place the pie on the lower shelf of the oven and bake for 40 minutes. Serve hot.

Gluten Free Basic Cheese

Makes 18 ounces

1 gallon milk
4 junket rennet tablets
2 tablespoons water

- Heat the milk to lukewarm. Crush the junket rennet tablets in a cup and dissolve in the water. Add the mixture to the lukewarm milk and stir well.
- Cover and set aside for 1 hour.
- Stir the firm milk to break the curds. Cover a large strainer with fine cheese cloth, place it over a bowl, and strain the curds, collecting the whey in a bowl.
  * The whey will be used to make fresh ricotta cheese.
- Place the cloth over a kitchen board. Squeeze and shape the cured with the help of the cloth into 2-inches thick squares.
- Press down on the cloth to drain all the remaining liquid.
- This basic cheese can be used in dessert recipes or salted and flavored to enjoy in sandwich or salads.

Gluten Free Ricotta Cheese

Makes 1 cup

3 cups whey (see recipe on page 171)
1 tablespoon lemon juice

- Place the whey in a glass bowl. Cover and allow the whey to sit for 12 hours at room temperature to increase the acid.
- Place the acid whey in a non-reactive and thick bottom pot. Stir in the lemon juice and start to heat the whey, stirring often, taking care to avoid sticking.
- Continue heating and stirring until white foam builds up and the whey is near boiling.
- Remove from the heat. Do not stir. Line a colander with a fine cloth. Gently and patiently spoon the curd into the cloth until you have spooned all the curd into the cloth and you have drained the yellowish liquid.
- Fold the cloth over the curd, place the colander over a bowl and put in the refrigerator. Allow the curd to drain for 6 hours or overnight.
- Remove the ricotta from the cloth and spoon into a container. You can use this ricotta in all recipes and you can also freeze until it is needed.

Gluten Free Vegetable Broth

Makes 6 cups

8 cups water
1 garlic clove, sliced
1 medium onion, chopped
1 celery stalk, chopped
1 carrot, diced
1 teaspoon sage
1 bay leave
potato peelings (if you have any)

- Place all ingredients in a large soup pot. Bring to a boil. Cover and simmer over low heat for 40 minutes.
- Strain the broth through a sauce strainer or through fine cloth. Discard the vegetables. You can refrigerate this broth for five days or keep it in the freezer for up six months.
- For storage, I recommend that you make thee separate freezer bags with two cups of broth in each bag. Because the broth can only be frozen for no longer than six months, you should use a Sharpie pen to label the bag with the kind of broth and the date it was frozen.

Gluten Free Beef Broth

Makes 6 cups

12 cups water
3 pounds meaty beef bones
2 celery stalk, chopped
1 medium onion, chopped
2 carrots, diced
1 garlic, sliced
1 bay leave
1 teaspoon black pepper
½ teaspoon nutmeg

- Place all ingredients in a heavy soup pot. Bring to a boil. Boil for 5 minutes. Cover and simmer for 3 hours.
- Remove from the heat; strain the broth through a sauce strainer or through a fine cloth.
- Discard the vegetables and the meat. Save the broth in the refrigerator for three days or keep in the freezer for up to six months.
- For storage, I recommend that you make thee separate freezer bags with two cups of broth in each bag. Because the broth can only be frozen for no longer than six months, you should use a Sharpie pen to label the bag with the kind of broth and the date it was frozen.

Gluten Free Chicken Broth

Makes 6 cups

12 cups water
2 pounds chicken wings, legs, and bones
1 medium onion, chopped
1 carrot, chopped
1 celery stalk
1 bay leave
1 clove

- Place all ingredients in a heavy soup pot. Bring to a boil. Boil for 5 minutes. Cover and simmer over low heat for 2 hours.
- Remove from the heat; strain the broth through sauce strainer or through a fine cloth.
- Discard the vegetables and the bones. Save the broth in the refrigerator for up to three days, or keep in the freezer for up to six months.
- For storage, I recommend that you make thee separate freezer bags with two cups of broth in each bag. Because the broth can only be frozen for no longer than six months, you should use a Sharpie pen to label the bag with the kind of broth and the date it was frozen.

BAKING AND DESSERTS

Corn Flat Bread

Makes 6 flat loaves

1 cup quinoa flakes
½ cup maize corn flour
¼ cup water
¼ teaspoon salt
½ teaspoon dry thyme
3 tablespoons olive oil

- Moisten the quinoa flakes with the water.
- Add the corn flour, salt, thyme and two tablespoons of olive oil. Mix well. Make into six balls.
- Moist your palms with the olive oil and flatten each ball into 4-inch flat bread.
- Place all bread on greased cookie sheet and bake in a 400 degree oven for 10 minutes or until golden.

Corn Bread

Makes 1 loaf

1¼ cups sweet white sorghum flour
1 cup yellow corn meal
¼ cup sugar
2 teaspoon baking powder
½ teaspoon salt
1 cup skim milk
¼ cup vegetable oil
¼ cup orange marmalade jam
1 egg

- Heat oven to 400 degrees.
- Grease a 9-inch pan.
- Mix the dry ingredients and set aside.
- Beat the egg with the sugar, then add the oil, milk and jam. Mix well.
- Add dry ingredients to the liquid mixture and mix until dry ingredients are fully moistened.
- Pour the batter into the pan and bake for 20-30 minutes or until light golden brown and knife inserted in the center comes out clean. Serve warm.

Kalamata Olive Bread

Makes 1 loaf

1 cup Kalamata olives, pitted and chopped
¼ cup olive oil
½ cup warm water
½ cup caramelized onions
1 tablespoon butter, melted
3 eggs
2 cups sweet white sorghum flour
1 teaspoon salt
½ teaspoon baking soda

- In a food processor, puree the olives, oil, butter, water and onion into a smooth puree. Set aside.
- Mix flours with salt and baking soda.
- Whisk the eggs, then add to the olive mixture.
- Gradually add the flour mixture to the egg-olive mixture and mix gently.
- Pour the batter into a greased bread pan. Bake in a 350 degree oven for 50 minutes or until crust is golden and knife inserted in bread comes out clean.
- Remove from the oven and allow to cool on a wire rack for 1 hour.

Rice Sandwich Bread

Makes 1 loaf

1½ cup white rice flour
1 cup brown rice flour
½ cup potato starch
½ cup sweet sorghum flour
3 tablespoons brown sugar
2⅓ teaspoons xanthan gum
1 teaspoon salt
2½ teaspoons yeast
1 cup warm milk
⅙ cup corn oil
⅔ teaspoon vinegar
2 eggs

- Mix the dry ingredients, except the yeast.
- Mix the sugar with the yeast and warm milk. Allow the yeast to rise.
- Whisk the egg with the corn oil, vinegar and the yeast mixture.
- Add the egg mixture to the dry mixture and mix gently. You should have sticky dough. Cover and allow the dough to rise for 45 minutes.
- Grease a 9x3 loaf pan, then spoon the dough into the pan. Cover and allow the dough to rest for another 30 minutes.
- Bake in a 375 degree oven for 45-60 minutes or until golden and knife inserted inside comes clean. Remove from the oven and allow the loaf to cool on rack. Remove from the pan and slice.

This recipe is adapted from Steve Schmidt of Baltic, South Dakota.

Onion Focaccia

Serves 8

1 dough rice sandwich bread
(see recipe on page 182)
4 tablespoons olive oil
2 red onions, thinly sliced
1 teaspoon rosemary, chopped
4 tablespoons fresh Parmesan cheese, grated

- Place the dough in a greased bowl, cover and allow it to rise for 1 hour.
- Rub the onions with two tablespoons of olive oil and the rosemary. Set aside.
- On a lightly floured surface, roll the dough into a 1-inch thick round.
- Place the dough on a greased pizza sheet or cookie sheet. Cover and allow the dough to rest for 30 minutes.
- Brush the top of the dough with the rest of the olive oil, then sprinkle on the onions.
- Bake in a 400 degree oven for 40-50 minutes or until crust is done and golden.
- Remove from the oven. Sprinkle the Parmesan cheese on top and enjoy warm or cold.

Pizza Crust (1) or Flat Bread

Makes 1 (12-inch) crust pizza or 4 flat loaves

- ½ cup Arborio rice
- 4 cups water
- ½ teaspoon salt
- 1 cup sweet sorghum flour
- 4 tablespoons olive oil

- Place rice with water and salt in a heavy saucepan. Bring to a boil. Turn the heat down and continue to cook on medium heat, stirring often until rice becomes sticky and starts to pull away from the sides. Remove from the stove and spoon into a bowl.
- Add the flour and two tablespoons of oil. Knead gently until all the flour is incorporated into the rice. Add a little more water if the dough is a bit dry.

To make pizza crust:

- Spread the dough on a greased pizza pan and bake in a 375 degree oven for 15 minutes. Remove from the oven.

To make flat bread:

- Grease your palms with the olive oil and divide the dough into four balls. Flatten each loaf to become a ⅛-inch thick flat and place on a greased cookie sheet. Bake in a 375 degree oven for 15 minutes. Remove from the oven and allow the bread to cool at room temperature. Wrap and refrigerate.

Pizza Crust (2)

Makes 1 (12-inch) crust

1 cup quinoa flakes
1 cup quinoa flour
1 cup Arborio rice
1 teaspoon salt
1 teaspoon baking soda
⅓ cup water
4 tablespoons olive oil
1 clove garlic, mashed

- Place the rice and four cups of water in a heavy saucepan and bring to a boil. Turn the heat down and cook, stirring often, until water evaporates and rice is sticky. Set aside.
- Preheat the oven to 400 degrees.
- Mix the quinoa flour, quinoa flakes, salt and baking soda.
- Mix the water with three tablespoons of olive oil and the garlic. Add to the flour mixture.
- Add the cooked Arborio and knead. If the dough is dry, add water until the dough is smooth.
- Grease a 12-inch pizza pan with olive oil, then press the dough into the pan. Drizzle the rest of the olive oil over the crust, then smooth the crust with your palm.
- Bake the crust for 10 minutes.
- Remove from the oven.

(Continued on next page)

To make pizza:

- Top the crust with tomato sauce, cheese and other toppings. Return to the oven and bake for another 20 minutes. Serve.

Zucchini Raisin Bread

Makes 2 loaves

2 cups garbanzo flour
1 cup rice flour
1 cup sugar
2 teaspoons cinnamon
1 teaspoon salt
1 tablespoon baking powder
1 teaspoon baking soda
3 large eggs
3 cups zucchini, shredded
2 cups raisins
1 cup walnuts, chopped
2 tablespoons vanilla
½ cup olive oil
1 cup skim milk

- Mix the dry ingredients together. Add the zucchini, raisins and nuts.
- In another bowl, beat together the eggs, vanilla, olive oil and skim milk.
- Pour the flour mixture over the oil batter and stir until it is thoroughly mixed.
- Pour batter into the loaf pans, about ⅔ full.
- Bake in a 350 degree oven for 1 hour or until a toothpick comes out clean.

Zucchini Almond Bread

Makes 2 loaves

3 cups sweet white sorghum flour
½ teaspoon salt
1 teaspoon baking soda
½ teaspoon baking powder
1 cup almonds, coarsely chopped and toasted
3 cups raw zucchini, grated
3 eggs
1½ cups sugar
½ cup orange marmalade
½ cup vegetable oil
1 tablespoon vanilla extract

- Preheat the oven to 350 degrees.
- Beat the eggs until light and foamy.
- Mix the flour with the rest of the dry ingredients.
- Add the sugar, oil, zucchini, and marmalade. Mix well.
- Add the dry ingredients to the egg-zucchini mixture. Stir until well blended. Pour into two 5x9x3 greased loaf pans.
- Bake in the oven for 50-60 minutes.

Sweet Potato Bread

Makes 1 loaf

1 cup pureed sweet potato
½ teaspoon ground cinnamon
½ teaspoon ground nutmeg
½ teaspoon ground cloves
1 tablespoon orange marmalade
¼ cup water
2 eggs
½ cup maple syrup
¼ cup vegetable oil
½ cup dark brown sugar
2½ cups sweet white sorghum flour
1 teaspoon baking soda
½ teaspoon salt

- In a microwave safe bowl, mix the sweet potato puree with the nutmeg, cinnamon, cloves, water and orange marmalade. Heat the mixture in the microwave for 1 minute.
- Whisk the eggs with the sugar and with the maple syrup, then add the oil. Whisk for a few seconds.
- Add the warm sweet potato mixture into the egg mixture and whisk until smooth.
- Mix the dry ingredients, then fold into the potato mixture until the components are mixed.
- Spoon batter into a greased 9-inch loaf pan.
- Bake in a 350 degree oven for 70 minutes. Remove from the oven and allow to cool at room temperature.

Cheese Bread

Makes 2 loaves

2 cups sweet white sorghum flour
1 cup quinoa flakes
1 cup rice flour
1 teaspoon baking soda
2 tablespoons xanthan gum
2 cups milk
1 tablespoon vinegar
2 eggs
¼ cup olive oil
1 cup Parmesan cheese
1 teaspoon rosemary

- Preheat oven to 400 degrees.
- Mix garbanzo flour, quinoa flakes and other dry ingredients, except for the gum.
- Warm the milk and mix with the xanthan gum.
- Whisk the eggs with the oil, add the warm milk and mix well.
- Add the egg-milk mixture to the dry ingredients and knead for 3 minutes, add a little water if the dough is dry, until the dough is velvety and a little sticky.
- Cut the dough in half and shape each piece into a log. Place on a baking sheet. Brush the loaves with egg white.
- Bake for 40 minutes. Remove and cool on a rack.

Crème Caramel

Serves 4

4 cups evaporated skim milk
1 cup sugar
½ cup orange marmalade
8 eggs

- In a heavy pan, mix ¾ cup of sugar with a half cup of water. Cook over high heat until the syrup turns brown—caramelized. Divide the caramelized syrup into four custard cups or ramekins.
- In a large bowl, mix skim milk with the eggs, the marmalade and the rest of the sugar, then pour it into the custard cups.
- Place the custard cups in a roasting pan and add enough hot water to the pan to reach halfway up the sides of the custard cups.
- Bake on the middle shelf of a 350 degree oven for 35 minutes.
- Remove the custard cups and chill for at least 4 hours.
- When ready to serve, slide a knife around the edge and turn the custard upside down, then serve.

Bread Pudding

Serves 6-8

4 cups evaporated skim milk
6 eggs
½ cup sugar
½ cup orange marmalade
1 tablespoon vanilla extract
1 cup raisins
6 slices rice sandwich bread, remove crust and cut into 1-inch cubes
zest of one lemon

- In a large bowl, whisk the milk, sugar and orange marmalade. Add the eggs, lemon zest and the vanilla extract.
- Add the corn bread and raisins to the milk mixture, cover and refrigerate for 1 hour.
- Pour the milk and bread mixture into 9x14 baking pan.
- Bake in a 350 degree oven for 1 hour.
- Remove from the oven. Allow the pudding to cool slightly, then serve.

Milk and Orange Pudding with Pistachio

Serves 4

4 cups 2% fat milk
1½ cups orange juice
1 cup sugar
5 tablespoons cornstarch
2 tablespoons orange blossom water* or vanilla extract
½ cup unsalted pistachios, crushed

Milk Pudding:

- Dissolve three tablespoons of cornstarch and half of the sugar in the milk.
- Heat the milk and simmer over medium-low heat, stirring constantly with a wooden spoon. When you feel resistance to the spoon and the mixture coats the spoon, turn off the heat. Stir one tablespoon of orange blossom water in the vanilla, then pour the pudding in four sundae dishes. Leave at least 1-inch from the top to make room for the orange pudding.
- Let the milk pudding cool for an hour before adding the orange pudding.

Orange Pudding:

- Dissolve the rest of the sugar and the rest of the cornstarch into the orange juice.
- Heat the orange mixture and simmer over medium heat, stirring constantly with a wooden spoon. When the mixture coats the spoon, stir in one tablespoon

(Continued on next page)

of the orange blossom water and turn off the heat. Allow the orange pudding to cool for 10 minutes.

- Slowly, pour a half-inch layer of orange pudding on top of the milk pudding.
- Chill overnight. Sprinkle with the pistachios and serve cold.

Hazelnut Tart

Serves 8

1 cup hazelnuts, coarsely chopped and toasted
1 stick unsalted butter
½ cup sugar
5 eggs
1 tablespoon vanilla extract
1 cup ricotta cheese (see recipe on page 172)
2 tablespoons dried apricots, chopped
¼ cup hazelnut flour
½ cup apricot preserves
2 tablespoons orange juice
zest of one lemon

- Grease a 9-inch round cheesecake pan with a removable bottom.
- Cream the butter and sugar until smooth. Separate the eggs and place the egg whites in a bowl and refrigerate.
- Mix the egg yolks with the butter-sugar mixture. Add the lemon zest, ricotta cheese, dried apricot, hazelnut flour and toasted hazelnuts.
- Beat the egg whites in a large bowl until stiff. Carefully, fold the egg whites into the ricotta mixture. Spoon this mixture into the baking pan, then bake in a 375 degree oven. Bake for 30-40 minutes. Let the cake cool on a rack.
- Remove the cake and place on a shallow serving pan. Heat the apricot jam with the orange juice, then drizzle over the cake. Serve.

Tiramisu

Serves 8

12 ounces lite tofu
12 ounces Mscarpon cheese
1 teaspoon vanilla extract
4 tablespoons maple syrup
1 loaf corn bread, cut into 1-inch thick slices
4 tablespoons Kahlua liqueur (optional)
1 cup strong coffee
2 teaspoons cocoa powder

- Place the cut corn bread on a tray and allow it to dry for at least 2 hours.
- In a food processor, puree tofu, vanilla extract and maple syrup into a smooth paste.
- Fold the tofu mixture into the cheese.
- Mix the coffee with the Kahlua.
- Quickly dip each corn bread stick into the coffee mixture. Do not soak them or they will fall apart.
- Place the dry side of each corn stick against the wall of a cheesecake pan with a removable bottom. Cover the bottom of the pan with the corn bread sticks.
- Spoon the tofu mixture inside the corn bread mold, cover with plastic wrap and refrigerate for 12 hours.
- Dust the top of the mold with the cocoa powder. Remove the edges of the pan and serve.

Corn Cannoli with Raspberry Sauce

Serves 6

12 fresh corn tortillas
1 tablespoon cornstarch
2 cups ricotta cheese (see recipe on page 172)
2 cups frozen raspberries, thawed
2 tablespoons sugar
zest of one lemon

•Mix the cornstarch with two tablespoons of water until you have a paste.

To make the filling:

• Whisk the ricotta cheese into smooth paste. Refrigerate.

To make the Cannoli Shells:

• Lightly spray twelve cannoli tubes with oil spray.
• Heat the corn tortillas, then wrap around the cannoli tubes. Glue with a dab of the cornstarch paste.
• Spray the outside of each cannoli with butter flavored spray. Place on a baking sheet and bake until golden and crisp, about 10 minutes.
• Remove from the oven and allow to cool for 10 minutes. Slide cannoli off the tubes and cool.

To make the sauce:

• Puree the raspberries in a food processor. Strain and whisk in the sugar and lemon zest.

(Continued on next page)

To serve:

- Fill the cannoli shell with the ricotta paste.
- Place two cannoli shells on a dessert plate. Drizzle with the raspberry sauce and serve.

Almond Sponge Cake

Serves 8

2 cups almond flour
1 cup quinoa flour
1 cup ground almonds, toasted
1 tablespoon baking powder
2 tablespoons xanthan Gum
1 cup sugar
6 tablespoons butter
3 eggs
½ cup orange marmalade
¼ cup orange juice
2 tablespoons powdered sugar for garnish
zest of one orange

- Preheat oven to 350 degrees.
- Grease a bundt cake pan.
- Mix both flours with the baking powder, gum and toasted almonds.
- In a chilled bowl, mix the butter and sugar until fluffy. Add the eggs one at a time. Stir in the flour mixture, orange marmalade, orange juice, and the orange zest. Spoon the mixture into the prepared baking pan.
- Bake in a preheated oven for 40-50 minutes or until an inserted knife comes out clean. Remove from the oven and allow to cool on a rack.
- Remove the cake from the pan, place on a shallow serving platter and dust with the powdered sugar. Serve.

Fig and Date Loaf

Serves 10

½ pound dried figs
½ pound pitted dates
1 cup walnuts, coarsely chopped
2 tablespoons honey
½ teaspoon ground cloves
½ teaspoon ground cardamom
2 tablespoons powdered sugar
1 tablespoon ground pistachios

- In a food processor, combine the figs with the dates and walnuts. Puree into a coarse mixture.
- Add the honey, cloves and cardamom and process into a smooth mixture.
- Spoon the mixture onto wax paper and shape into 3-inch thick cylinders.
- Chill for a couple of hours.

When ready to serve:

- Remove the wax paper, cut into 1-inch thick slices, then sprinkle with the powdered sugar and the pistachios.

Cinnamon Biscotti

Makes about 30 biscotti

- 2½ cups sweet white sorghum flour
- 3 teaspoons ground cinnamon
- 1 teaspoon baking powder
- ¼ teaspoon salt
- 1 cup sugar
- 6 tablespoons unsalted butter, room temperature
- 3 large eggs
- ½ cup orange marmalade
- 1 teaspoon vanilla extract

- Preheat the oven to 325 degrees.
- Mix flour, two teaspoons cinnamon, baking powder and salt.
- With an electric mixer, beat all the sugar, except for two tablespoons, and the butter until fluffy.
- Add two eggs and beat well. Mix in vanilla extract and orange marmalade.
- Add the flour-cinnamon mixture and mix well. Divide the dough in half.
- Shape each half into a 9-inch long log.
- Transfer logs to a parchment lined cookie sheet.
- Beat remaining egg in a small bowl, brush logs with the egg wash.
- Bake in the preheated oven for 40 minutes.
- Remove from the oven and cool for 15 minutes. Maintain oven temperature.
- Mix the rest of the sugar with the rest of the cinnamon.

(Continued on next page)

- Using a serrated knife, cut the log at a 35 degree angle into half inch thick slices.
- Place biscotti, cut side down, on a baking sheet.
- Sprinkle cinnamon-sugar mixture over each biscotti. Bake for 15 minutes. Remove from the oven and cool on a rack. Serve.

Pistachio Biscotti

Makes 24 biscotti

1½ cups almond flour
½ cup soy flour
4 tablespoons unsalted butter, softened
1½ cups orange marmalade
1 cup brown sugar, packed
1 egg
½ cup ground almonds, toasted
1 teaspoon baking powder
1 teaspoon vanilla extract
½ teaspoon cinnamon
¼ teaspoon salt
1 cup shelled unsalted pistachios

- Preheat the oven to 325 degrees.
- In a food processor, beat the butter and the sugar until creamy.
- Add the orange marmalade and vanilla extract and continue to mix.
- Add the egg, beat well.
- Add the flour, ground almonds, baking powder, cinnamon and salt. Beat thoroughly.
- Divide the dough into two parts and shape each part into a 12-inch long log.
- Place both logs on a cookie sheet. Set them three-inches apart.
- Refrigerate for 2 hours.
- Bake for 35 minutes, or until they are dry to the touch.
- Let cool for about 30 minutes, then diagonally cut the logs into half inch thick slices.

(Continued on next page)

- Arrange the biscotti on the cookie sheet next to each other. Bake for 20 minutes.
- Remove from the oven and cool on a rack for an hour.
- The biscotti can be stored in a covered cookie tin for 1 week.

Carrot Cake

Makes 16 servings

- 1 pound carrots, enough to make 1½ cups after they are boiled and mashed
- 2 cups soy flour
- 1½ cups sugar
- 2 teaspoons baking powder
- 1 teaspoon baking soda
- 1 teaspoon cinnamon
- 1 teaspoon nutmeg
- 1 teaspoon cardamom
- ½ teaspoon salt
- 1 cup orange marmalade
- 4 eggs
- 1 cup raisins
- ½ cup walnuts, chopped
- 4 cloves
- 4 whole cardamom seeds

- Preheat the oven to 375 degrees.
- In a heavy pot, cover the carrots, cloves and cardamom in water and boil until the carrots are soft.
- Drain the carrots; discard the cloves and the cardamom. Puree the carrots in a food processor.
- In a large bowl, combine the pureed carrots with the rest of the ingredients, except for the nuts and raisins.
- Beat at low speed for 4 minutes. Gently stir in the nuts and raisins.
- Grease a 9x13 pan.
- Pour into the greased pan and bake for 45-60 minutes or until a toothpick inserted in the center comes out clean. Remove from the oven and cool completely.

Chocolate Bars

Makes 24 bars

1 cup soy flour
1 cup orange marmalade
4 ounces lite silken tofu, pureed
6 ounces unsweetened chocolate, chopped
3 eggs
¾ cup sugar
¼ cup olive oil
2 teaspoons vanilla extract
½ cup semisweet chocolate chips
1 tablespoon powdered sugar

- Grease a 9x13x2 metal baking pan.
- Preheat oven to 350 degrees.
- Place the olive oil and chopped chocolate in a small bowl. Place the bowl on top of boiling water, stir until chocolate is melted and mixture is smooth. Remove from heat.
- In a large bowl, whisk eggs and sugar until pale yellow, about 3 minutes. Gradually add and whisk in the warm chocolate mixture.
- Add the orange marmalade, pureed tofu and vanilla extract.
- Mix in the flour, then the chocolate chips.
- Pour batter into the greased baking pan. Bake for 25 minutes or until a toothpick inserted in the center comes out with moist crumbs attached. Remove from the oven and cool completely on a rack.
- Cut into 2-inch squares. Sift powdered sugar on top and serve.

Raisin Cornmeal Cookies

Makes 3 dozen cookies

1½ cups soy flour
1 cup yellow cornmeal
½ cup sugar
¾ cup dark raisins
2 eggs, room temperature
4 tablespoons unsalted butter
½ cup apple butter
½ cup orange preserves
1 teaspoon ground anise seeds
2 teaspoons baking powder
dash of salt

- Soak the raisins in hot water for 30 minutes, drain and toss with one tablespoon of soy flour.
- Beat the butter, sugar, apple butter and orange preserves until it becomes a smooth paste.
- Add the eggs, one at a time. Beat after each addition.
- In a bowl, mix soy flour, cornmeal, anise seeds, baking powder and salt. Add the flour mixture to the egg-butter mixture and mix thoroughly. Add the raisins and mix.
- Transfer the dough to a lightly floured surface. Divide the dough into two balls. Roll each ball into a 2-inch thick log.
- Slice the log in half inch thick rounds.
- Place cookies on a greased cookie sheet about 2-inches apart.
- Bake in a 375 degree oven until lightly browned, about 20 minutes.
- Remove from the oven and cool on a rack.

Basic Tart Dough

Makes 8 mini tarts or 2 (9-inch) tarts

1½ cups sweet white sorghum flour
½ cup rice flour
½ cup brown sugar
1½ sticks unsalted butter, room temperature
2 eggs
1 teaspoon vanilla extract
zest of two lemons
pinch of salt

- Cream the butter and sugar until pale and creamy. Add the eggs, vanilla and lemon zest and beat until well blended.
- Scrape down the sides of the bowl. Add both flours and beat until the dough forms a sticky ball.
- Shape the dough into a disk and wrap well in plastic. Refrigerate for at least an hour.
- Remove the dough from the refrigerator and place on a floured surface. Cut the dough into eight pieces. Roll each piece into 5-inch rounds.
- Gently place the rounds inside tart pans with removable bottoms. Press gently inside the bottom of the ring to form a nice mold. Place the tart pans on a cookie sheet and chill for 30 minutes.
- Place the cookie sheet in the middle of a 375 degree oven and bake. Bake 10 minutes for partially baked shells or 15 minutes for fully baked shells.
- Remove from the oven and cool completely in the tart pan before removing from the tart pans.

Basic Chocolate Tart Dough

1 cup white sweet sorghum flour
½ cup rice flour
½ cup unsweetened Dutch processed cocoa powder
10 tablespoons unsalted butter, room temperature
½ cup sugar
1 egg
1 tablespoon vanilla

- Sift together the flours and cocoa powder.
- Cream the sugar and butter until pale yellow and creamy. Add the egg and vanilla and beat until well blended.
- Scrape the side of the bowl, then add the flour-cocoa mixture and beat until the dough forms a sticky mass.
- Shape the dough into a disk and wrap well in plastic and refrigerate for 2 hours.
- Remove the dough from the refrigerator and place on a floured surface. Cut the dough into eight pieces. Roll each piece into 5-inch rounds.
- Gently place each round inside tart pan with a removable bottom. Press gently inside the bottom of the ring to form a nice mold. Place the tart pans on a cookie sheet and chill for 30 minutes.
- Place the cookie sheet in the middle of a 375 degree oven and bake. Bake 10 minutes for partially baked shells or 15 minutes for fully baked shells.
- Remove from the oven and cool completely in the tart pan before removing from the tart pans.

Apricot and Pistachio Tarts

Makes 8 tarts

8 partially baked tart shells
2 cups ricotta cheese
1 tablespoon sugar
1 10-ounce can of apricots, drained and chopped
2 tablespoons pistachios, finely ground

- Mix the ricotta with the sugar and apricots.
- Spoon the ricotta mixture inside the tart shells.
- Bake in a 375 degree oven for 10 minutes. Remove from the oven and cool slightly.
- Sprinkle with pistachios and serve.

Fig and Chocolate Tarts

Makes 8 tarts

8 partially baked chocolate tart shells
1 cup sweetened coconut milk
2 cups dried figs, chopped
1 cup unsweetened shredded coconut
½ teaspoon ground anise seeds
1 teaspoon corn starch

- Mix the corn starch with the coconut milk.
- Toss figs with the shredded coconuts and ground anise seeds.
- Add the coconut milk to the fig mixture and mix well.
- Place the tart shells on a cookie sheet. Divide the fig mixture evenly among the tart shells.
- Bake in a 350 degree oven for 20 minutes, or until the coconut is lightly toasted. Remove from the oven and allow tarts to cool 30 minutes before serving.

Chocolate and Strawberry Tarts

Makes 8 tarts

8 fully baked chocolate tarts
2 cups whipped cream
8 strawberries
2 tablespoons sweet chocolate, finely shaved

- Place each tart on a white serving dish.
- Spoon whipped cream inside each tart.
- Place one strawberry, with its cap still on, upright on each tart.
- Sprinkle the shaved chocolate over and around each tart and serve.

Nammoraa, Corn and Coconut Bars

Makes about 20 bars

2 tablespoons Tahini*
4 cups yellow corn meal
1 cup unsweetened shredded coconuts
1 cup sugar
½ cup melted butter
2 cups plain yogurt
1 teaspoon baking powder
½ teaspoon baking soda
3 cups honey

- Mix corn meal, coconuts, sugar and butter.
- Mix yogurt with baking soda and baking powder. Add the corn meal mixture and blend into a smooth paste.
- Grease 12x17 pan with Tahini. Pour the mixture into the pan and smooth the top. Cut into 2-inch wide bars.
- Bake in a 400 degree oven for 30 minutes, or until brown.
- Pour the honey on top and allow to cool before serving.

Sweet Potato Cookies

Makes 14 cookies

1 medium yam, baked
4 ounces raspberry jam
½ cup soy flour
1 teaspoon baking powder
¼ teaspoon cardamom
½ cup raisins
¼ cup sugar
2 eggs
1 tablespoon olive oil
zest of one lemon

- Peel the baked yam and mash it. You should have about ¾ cup of mashed yam.
- Whisk the eggs with the sugar and olive oil. Add the raspberry jam and lemon zest. Add the yam and mix well.
- Mix the dry ingredients and add to the yam mixture. Mix well.
- Fold in the raisins.
- Drop about a tablespoon of dough onto a cookie sheet.
- Bake in a 375 degree oven for 30 minutes.

Double Chocolate Scones

Makes 10

- 1 cup soy flour
- 2 cups hazelnut flour
- ⅓ cup unsweetened cocoa powder
- ½ cup brown sugar, packed
- ½ cup olive oil
- ⅓ cup orange preserves
- 8 ounces non-fat plain yogurt
- 2 teaspoons baking powder
- 1 teaspoon baking soda
- ¼ teaspoon salt
- 1 egg yolk, beaten
- ½ cup semisweet chocolate chips
- 1 teaspoon powdered sugar (optional)

- Preheat oven to 350 degrees.
- In a large bowl stir together flour, cocoa powder, brown sugar, baking powder, baking soda and salt.
- Add olive oil and mix until mixture resembles coarse crumbs.
- Combine egg yolk, yogurt and orange preserves.
- Add yogurt mixture into the dry ingredients. Mix well.
- Add chocolate chips. Stir mixture until moistened.
- On a lightly floured surface, gently knead dough until dough is nearly smooth.
- Pat dough into a 9-inch circle; cut into ten wedges.
- Place wedges 1-inch apart on an ungreased baking sheet.
- Bake for 30 minutes.

(Continued on next page)

- Remove from the baking sheet; cool on a wire rack for 5 minutes.
- Dust top with powdered sugar. Serve warm.

Coffee Raspberry Brownies

Makes 24 brownies

½ cup unsalted butter, room temperature
4 ounces bitter chocolate, coarsely chopped
2 large eggs
1 cup sugar
¼ cup orange marmalade
¼ cup raspberry preserves
1 cup hazelnut flour
½ teaspoon baking powder
¼ teaspoon salt
1 cup chocolate covered espresso beans, coarsely ground

- Grease and lightly flour a 9-inch square baking pan.
- In a small heavy saucepan, melt butter, add the chocolate and melt over low heat. Whisk until a smooth paste. Remove from heat.
- Whisk the eggs and sugar. Add the marmalade and the raspberry jam. Whisk well. Add the melted chocolate.
- Mix the flour with the baking powder, salt and chocolate espresso beans. Add flour mixture into the chocolate batter and beat well.
- Spread the batter evenly in a pan and bake in the middle of a 350 degree oven for 30 minutes, or until a tester comes out with crumbs.
- Cool brownies completely in the pan on a rack before cutting into 24 squares.

Cocoa Brownies

Makes 20 pieces

- 1 cup sweet white sorghum flour
- ⅓ cup tapioca flour
- ⅓ cup coconut flour
- ¾ cup baking cocoa powder
- ½ teaspoon baking powder
- ½ teaspoon salt
- ¾ cup unsalted butter
- 1 cup brown sugar
- ¼ cup sugar
- ½ cup orange marmalade
- 2 eggs
- 2 tablespoons vanilla extract
- 1 cup semisweet chocolate chips

- Preheat oven to 350 degree.
- Mix sugars with the butter. Stir in the eggs, orange marmalade and vanilla extract.
- Mix the dry ingredients and add to the egg mixture. Mix well.
- Spread into greased 9x13 baking pan. Sprinkle the chocolate chips on top and press gently.
- Bake for 20 minutes. Remove from the oven and allow to cool before cutting the brownies.

Fudge Brownies with Chocolate Chips

Serves 24

- 1 cup soy flour
- 1 cup orange marmalade
- 4 ounces lite silken tofu, pureed
- 4 ounces unsweetened chocolate, chopped
- 3 eggs
- ½ cup sugar
- ¼ cup olive oil
- 2 teaspoons vanilla extract
- ½ cup semisweet chocolate chips
- 1 tablespoon powdered sugar

- Grease a 9x13x2 metal baking pan.
- Preheat oven to 350 degrees.
- Place olive oil and chopped chocolate in a small metal bowl. Place the bowl on top of boiling water, stir until chocolate is melted and mixture is smooth. Remove from heat.
- In a large bowl, whisk eggs and sugar until pale yellow, about 3 minutes.
- Gradually whisk in the warm chocolate mixture.
- Whisk in orange marmalade, tofu and vanilla extract.
- Mix in the flour, then chocolate chips.
- Pour batter into a greased baking pan.
- Bake brownies for 25 minutes. A knife inserted in the center should come out with moist crumbs attached.
- Cool brownies completely in the pan on a rack.
- Cut into squares. Sift powdered sugar on top.

Chocolate Chunk Cookies

Makes 20 cookies

8 ounces semi-sweet chocolate squares
⅓ cup brown sugar, firmly packed
2 tablespoons unsalted butter
1 egg
1 tablespoon vanilla extract
½ cup sorghum flour
¼ cup tapioca flour
¼ teaspoon baking powder
½ teaspoon salt
1 cup walnuts, chopped

- Preheat oven to 350 degrees.
- Coarsely chop half of the chocolate squares into small chunks. Set aside.
- Microwave the remaining chocolate squares in a bowl for 1 minute. Stir and heat for another minute or until chocolate is completely melted.
- Add the sugar, butter, eggs and vanilla extract. Mix well.
- Mix the flours with the baking powder and salt. Stir the flour mixture in to the egg-chocolate mixture. Mix well.
- Stir in the chocolate chunks and the walnuts.
- Spoon one tablespoon of the dough, two inches apart, onto an ungreased cookie sheet.
- Bake for 12 minutes. Remove from the oven and cool for 10 minutes. Remove cookies from the cookie sheet and cool completely on a rack before serving.

Chocolate Coconut Cake

Makes 12 servings

6 ounces bittersweet baking chocolate
¾ cup unsalted butter
¼ cup orange marmalade
1 cup sorghum flour
½ cup coconut flour
½ teaspoon baking powder
4 eggs
½ cup sugar

- Heat oven to 350 degrees.
- Mix both flours with the baking powder.
- Place chocolate with the butter in a microwave safe bowl. Microwave for a couple of minutes. Remove from the microwave and stir well. Set aside.
- Beat the sugar with the eggs until thickened. Add the marmalade and the chocolate mix. Blend well.
- Add the flour mixture, stir until well blended.
- Pour into greased and floured 9-inch cake pan.
- Bake in the oven for 30 minutes or until center is set. Remove from the oven and cool completely.

Poached Pears

Serves 8

4 Bosc pears, peeled and cut in half lengthwise
2 cups dry red wine
1 cup sugar
1 cup cranberry juice
½ cup dried cranberries
zest of one lemon

- In a large stainless steel saucepan, combine all the ingredients, except the pears. Bring to a boil.
- Reduce heat. Place the pears cut side down in the pan and simmer for 20 minutes.
- Gently remove the pears and continue to simmer the wine sauce until it reduces to half its volume.
- Place the pears cut side down on a white serving platter. Pour the wine sauce over and around the pears. Chill for a couple of hours before serving.

Apricot Tarts

Serves 8

For the crust:

½ cup soy flour
½ cup almond flour
⅓ cup yellow corn meal
2 tablespoons olive oil
1 egg
⅓ cup sugar
¼ cup water
1 tablespoon vanilla extract

For the filling:

10 ounces lite tofu
⅓ cup sugar
1 tablespoon vanilla extract
1 can apricot halves in light syrup
1 teaspoon sugar
½ teaspoon cinnamon

- Preheat the oven to 375 degrees.
- In a food processor, process all crust ingredients until the mixture resembles coarse meal.
- Lightly grease 9-inch flan pan with olive oil spray.
- Place the dough in the center of the pan and press it until the dough covers the bottom and along the sides.
- Trim the pastry using a sharp knife.
- Bake for 25 minutes or until golden.
- Drain the apricots and set aside.

(Continued on next page)

- In a food processor, puree tofu with sugar and vanilla extract.

To assemble the tart:

- Mix cinnamon and sugar.
- Spoon the tofu cream into the baked tart.
- Arrange apricots, cut side down, over the tofu cream, then sprinkle with the cinnamon sugar.

Apricot Sour Cream Scones

Serves 8

1 cup soy flour
½ cup coconut flour
½ cup brown sugar, packed
2 teaspoons baking powder
1 teaspoon baking soda
½ teaspoon salt
¼ cup olive oil
⅓ cup apricot butter
¼ cup orange preserves
½ cup low-fat sour cream
1 tablespoon vanilla extract
½ cup dried apricots, chopped
1 egg white, beaten for glaze
1 teaspoon brown sugar

- Preheat oven to 375 degrees.
- In a large bowl, mix flours, brown sugar, baking powder, baking soda and salt.
- Add olive oil, apricot butter and orange preserves.
- Blend together with fingertips until mixture resembles coarse meal.
- Add sour cream and vanilla extract to the flour mixture and mix until the dough is nearly smooth.
- Place the dough on a lightly floured surface.
- Sprinkle the apricots over the dough and knead until the apricots are incorporated.
- Flatten the dough into an 8-inch round. Cut into eight wedges.

(Continued on next page)

- Transfer the wedges to a baking sheet. Brush with the egg white, then sprinkle with the brown sugar.
- Bake for 25 minutes.
- Serve warm.

Sweet Pizza

Serves 6

- 6 ounces lite tofu, pureed
- 1 cup coconut flour
- 1 cup sweet white sorghum flour
- ½ cup rice flour
- ½ cup apple juice
- ½ cup plain soy milk
- 3 tablespoons brown sugar
- 1 teaspoon ground anise seeds
- 1 tablespoon cinnamon
- ¼ cup water

- Mix all flours with brown sugar, anise seeds and cinnamon.
- Mix tofu with the apple juice, soy milk and water. Add the dry ingredients and mix well. Knead until the dough is smooth. Add a little juice if the dough is dry.
- Line the cookie sheet with parchment paper and roll the dough on it.
- Bake in a 400 degree oven for 40 minutes or until golden.
- Cut and serve hot.

Almond Apricot Cakes

Makes 12 mini cakes

- 3 tablespoons unsalted butter
- ¼ cup sugar
- 2 tablespoons almond paste
- ¼ teaspoon vanilla extract
- 1 egg
- 3 tablespoons sweet white sorghum flour
- ⅛ teaspoon salt
- 12 dried apricots
- 1 tablespoon honey
- 1 cup orange juice
- zest of one orange

- Brush muffin cups with butter and lightly dust with flour.
- Beat sugar and butter until fluffy. Beat in the almond paste and vanilla extract. Add the egg and beat well.
- Mix flour with the salt, then fold into the egg mixture and mix until just combined.
- Spoon batter evenly into the muffin cups.
- Bake in a 400 degree oven until edges are golden, about 15 minutes.
- Remove from the oven and cool on a wire rack. Remove the cakes and place on a flat serving platter.
- In a small saucepan, bring the orange juice and honey to a boil. Drop in the apricots and the orange zest, then simmer for 5 minutes. Remove from the heat and spoon one apricot with a little sauce on top of each muffin.

Almond Cookies

Makes 3 dozen

1 cup soy flour
1 cup almond flour
6 ounces lite tofu
3 large eggs
2 tablespoons orange blossom water
2 cup almonds
1 teaspoon cardamom
¼ teaspoon salt

- Preheat oven to 400 degrees.
- Butter and lightly dust with flour a 9x13x2 metal baking pan.
- Mix flours, cardamom and salt in a bowl.
- In a food processor, mix sugar, tofu, eggs and orange blossom water until blended well.
- Add half of the flour mixture and blend well until mixed. Add the rest of the flour mixture and blend well.
- Spoon the batter into a bowl. Stir in the almonds.
- Spoon the batter into the greased baking pan.
- Spray your palm with canola oil, and then with the palm smooth the top of the batter.
- Bake for 20 minutes.
- Cool for 10 minutes. Turn the pastry onto a rack and cool for 1 hour.
- Place the pastry on a board and cut crosswise into half inch wide strips.
- Cut each strip diagonally into three pieces.

(Continued on next page)

- Arrange cookies, cut side down, on baking sheets.
- Bake until cookies are golden brown, about 10 minutes.
- Transfer cookies to a rack and cool for a couple of hours.

Celestial Cake

Serves 12

For the cake:

- 1½ cups sweet white sorghum flour
- 12 ounces lite tofu
- 1½ cups sugar
- 4 eggs
- ½ cup orange preserves
- ¼ cup olive oil
- 2 teaspoons vanilla extract
- 1 teaspoon baking powder

For the topping:

- 8 ounces part-skim ricotta cheese
- 8 ounces cream cheese
- ¼ cup orange preserves
- 2 cups crushed pineapple, drained

To make the cake:

- Preheat oven to 325 degrees.
- Grease and lightly flour two 9-inch round cake pans.
- Mix flour and baking powder.
- In a food processor, mix tofu, sugar, eggs, orange preserves, olive oil and vanilla extract. Mix until well blended. Spoon the egg mixture into a bowl.
- Add the flour mixture to the egg mixture and mix until fully combined.
- Divide the batter between the two greased pans. Spread the batter evenly in each pan.

(Continued on next page)

- Bake for 30 minutes or until a wooden toothpick inserted near the center comes out clean.
- Cool on a rack for 1 hour.

To make the topping:
- In a chilled bowl, whip the cream cheese and the ricotta cheese together.
- Add the orange preserves and crushed pineapple to the cheese mixture. Fold gently until well blended. Chill for 30 minutes.

To assemble the cake:
- Place the first cake on a cake serving platter.
- Spread ⅓ of the pineapple cheese topping on top of the cake.
- Place the second cake on top of the first cake.
- Spread the rest of topping on top and around the edges to cover both cakes.
- Refrigerate for 1 hour before serving.

Apricot Squares

Makes 24

1 cup almond flour
1 cup soy flour
½ cup hazelnut flour
¾ cup unsalted butter
4 tablespoons sugar
1 tablespoon orange blossom water (optional)
⅔ cup quinoa flour
1½ cups dried apricots, finely chopped
2 cups light brown sugar
4 large eggs
2 tablespoons vanilla extract
¼ teaspoon salt
¼ cup orange marmalade
2 cups walnuts, coarsely chopped and toasted

To make the crust:

- Mix almond flour with soy flour, hazelnut flour and sugar.
- Add the butter and orange blossom water and gently mix until butter and flours are well mixed.
- Press the dough into 9x16 baking pan.
- Bake in a 350 degree oven for 10 minutes. Remove from the oven and cool for 10 minutes.

To make the squares:

- Mix quinoa flour with the brown sugar, salt and apricot.

(Continued on next page)

- Whisk the eggs with the orange marmalade and vanilla extract. Add the flour mixture and mix well. Pour this mixture over the baked crust.
- Spread the toasted walnuts on top of the batter and press gently with a spatula into the batter.
- Bake in a 350 degree oven for 35 minutes.
- Remove from the oven and cool for a couple of hours before cutting.
- Cut into 2-inch squares and serve.

Date Bars

Makes 12 bars

- ½ cup unsalted butter
- ½ cup quinoa flour
- 1 cup hazelnut flour
- 2 tablespoons white sugar
- 1 teaspoon ground cardamom
- 1½ cups brown sugar
- 1 cup pecans, chopped
- 8 ounces dates, chopped
- 3 eggs
- 3 tablespoons soy flour
- ½ teaspoon baking soda
- 1 tablespoon vanilla extract
- ¼ teaspoon salt

To make the crust:

- Mix quinoa flour with the hazelnut flour, white sugar and cardamom. Add the butter and blend until you have coarse dough.
- Press the dough firmly into the bottom of a 9-inch square cake pan.
- Bake the dough in a 350 degree oven for 10 minutes. Remove from the oven and allow to cool for 15 minutes.

To make the bars:

- Mix the brown sugar with the chopped pecans, chopped dates, the rest of the flour, baking soda and salt.

(Continued on next page)

- Whisk the eggs and vanilla extract, and then add to the date mixture. Mix until well blended.
- Pour the date batter over the baked crust. Tap the baking pan gently.
- Bake in a 375 degree oven for 35 minutes.
- Remove from the oven, place on a rack and allow it to cool for a couple hours.
- Refrigerate for 30 minutes. Cut into 2-inch squares.

Maamoul—Walnut Stuffed Cookies

Makes 30 cookies

3 cups walnuts
1 cup sugar
2 tablespoons orange blossom water
4 cups yellow cornmeal
2 cups white sweet sorghum flour
3 cups unsalted butter
1 teaspoon salt
1 teaspoon yeast
¾ cup warm milk
½ cup powdered sugar

To make the stuffing:

- Place the walnuts, sugar and orange blossom water in a food processor and grind until it is a fine mixture. Spoon into a bowl and set aside.

To make the maamoul dough:

- Dissolve the yeast in the warm milk. Allow to set for a couple of minutes.
- In a chilled bowl, mix both flours with the butter and the yeast mixture. Add more milk if the dough is dry.

Making the Maamoul:

- Divide the dough into walnut size balls. Smooth the balls round with the palm of your hand. With the forefinger, make a hole in dough and shape into a small cup like shape.

(Continued on next page)

- Spoon about a teaspoon of the filling into the cup and gently close the opening with your fingers. Place the closed side on a cookie sheet and gently flatten the bottom. You should have a dome shaped cookie. Decorate with the tip of a fork. Repeat these steps until you stuff and shape all the balls.
- Bake in a 300 degree oven for 40 minutes, or until golden on the bottom of the cookies.
- Remove from the oven, allow the cookies to cool for 1 hour, then dust with powdered sugar.

Sesame Walnut Bars

Makes 24 bars

- 1½ cups sweet white sorghum flour
- 1 cup quinoa flour
- 1 cup packed brown sugar
- 1 teaspoon baking soda
- ¼ teaspoon salt
- ¾ cup unsalted butter
- 2 cups sesame seeds, toasted in a 350 degree oven for 8 minutes
- 1 cup roasted unsalted peanuts
- ½ cup walnuts, toasted
- 2 cups sugar
- 1 cup water
- 1 tablespoon lemon juice

- Combine both flours with the brown sugar, baking soda, salt and butter. Stir until all ingredients are moistened.
- Press mixture into bottom of an ungreased 9x13 baking pan.
- Bake in a 350 degree oven for 15 minutes. Remove from the oven and allow to cool completely.
- In a heavy pot, bring water, sugar and lemon juice into a boil. Cook over medium heat until it becomes thick and sticky. Remove from heat, stir in the nuts and spread over the baked crust.
- Cool completely, then cut into 2-inch squares.

Rice Pudding

Serves 8

½ cup almonds, slivered
½ cup walnuts, coarsely chopped
½ cup pistachios
½ cup short rice
5 cups 2% milk
¼ cup rice flour
½ cup raisins
½ cup sugar
2 tablespoons orange blossom water
1 teaspoon caraway seeds, crushed
½ teaspoon cinnamon
½ ground anise seeds

- Place the almonds, walnuts and pistachios in a bowl and cover with cold water. Allow the nuts to soak in water for at least 2 hours before using them.
- In a large heavy pot, cook the short rice in 1½ cups of water until the rice is soft, but not mushy.
- Add the milk, sugar and rice flour to the cooked rice. Stir and cook over medium-low heat for 5 minutes.
- Add the cinnamon, caraway seeds, anise and raisins. Stir and bring the mixture to a simmer, stirring continuously, until thickened.
- Pour the milk mixture into eight custard cups. Cool for 15 minutes, then refrigerate for a couple of hours or overnight.
- When ready to serve, drain the mixed nuts. Sprinkle the top of the pudding with the nuts and serve.

Almond Orange Cake

Serves 8

- 4 tablespoons butter
- 1 cup sugar
- ¼ cup almond paste
- ¼ teaspoon vanilla extract
- 3 eggs
- ½ cup sweet white sorghum flour
- ½ cup hazelnut flour
- ⅛ teaspoon salt

For the orange sauce:

- 1 orange
- 1 tablespoon butter
- ¼ cup sugar
- ¼ cup orange liquor (Cointreau)

To make the cake:

- Cream the sugar with the butter. Add the almond paste and vanilla extract. Mix well.
- Whisk the eggs, then add to the sugar mixture.
- Mix the dry ingredients and add to the egg mixture. Mix gently.
- Grease a 9-inch round cake pan. Spoon the batter into the cake pan.
- Bake in a 400 degree oven for 15-20 minutes or until a knife inserted comes out clean.
- Remove from the oven.

(Continued on next page)

To make the orange sauce:

- Thinly peel the orange. Avoid the white skin. Cut the orange peel into very thin strips.
- Heat the butter and sauté the orange peel for 1 minute. Squeeze the orange and pour the orange juice over the orange peels.
- Add the sugar and orange liqueur. Bring to a boil, then simmer for 10 minutes.
- Remove from heat and pour the warm sauce over the cake.
- Serve the cake warm or cold.

Rice Kenafeh

Serves 8

- 8 ounces rice noodles
- 4 cups skim milk
- ¼ cup sugar
- 1 tablespoon unsalted butter
- 12 ounces ricotta cheese (see recipe on page 172)
- 1 tablespoon vanilla or orange blossom water
- 1 cup maple syrup or honey

- Preheat the oven to 400 degrees.
- In a bowl, whisk the ricotta cheese with the sugar and vanilla extract.
- In a heavy sauce pan, bring the milk, ricotta and sugar mixture to a boil. Bread the rice noodles and drop into the boiling milk. Turn the heat down and continue to boil for 3 minutes, stirring often.
- Remove from heat, drain and toss the noodles gently with the butter.
- Line 5x9 or 9-inch pan with parchment paper. Spread the noodle mixture in the pan.
- Bake on the bottom shelf of the oven for 15 minutes or until light golden on the edges. Remove from the oven.
- Spoon the whipped ricotta mixture in a 5x9 or 9-inch serving pan. Turn the baked noodles upside down over the whipped ricotta. Remove the pan and the parchment paper.
- Drizzle with maple syrup or honey and serve warm.

Chocolate Chip Cookies

Makes 3 dozen

2 sticks unsalted butter
½ cup granulated sugar
¾ cup brown sugar, packed
½ cup orange marmalade
1 tablespoon vanilla extract
2 eggs
¼ cup milk
½ cup rice flour
2 cups sweet white sorghum flour
1 teaspoon baking powder
½ teaspoon salt
2 cups milk chocolate chips

- Mix both flours with the baking powder and salt.
- In a bowl, beat the butter with the sugars and orange marmalade. Add the eggs and vanilla and beat until creamy.
- Add the flour mixture and mix until well blended.
- Stir in the chocolate chips.
- For each cookie, spoon one tablespoon on a cookie sheet and spread gently with the back of the spoon.
- Bake in a 375 degree oven for 10 minutes. Cool the cookies on a rack completely before moving them.

This recipe is adopted from a Hershey's chocolate chip recipe.

Butter Sugar Cookies

Makes 2 dozen

1 stick unsalted butter
½ cup powder sugar
¼ cup instant nonfat dry milk
¼ cup almond paste
½ cup sweet white sorghum flour
½ cup coconut flour
1 teaspoon orange blossom water

- Beat butter and sugar with an electric mixer until white and creamy.
- Add the almond paste, dry milk and orange blossom water and beat until well blended.
- Add the rest of the ingredients and mix well.
- Make 24 balls. Flatten each ball into 2-inch circles and place on a cookie sheet.
- Bake in a 375 degree oven for 10 minutes. Remove from the oven and cool completely before serving.

Glossary

Harrisa: North African Hot Red Pepper Paste. Harrisa is available in Middle Eastern and North African groceries.

Kasha: These are buckwheat groats that have been toasted in oil to remove buckwheat's natural bitterness and to bring a sweet nutty flavor. You can use kasha for any recipe that calls for bulgur. Kasha is generally available in any Health food store.

Pomegranate Molasses: Concentrated syrup distilled from pomegranate juice, available in Middle Eastern groceries.

Quinoa: Native to the Andes, quinoa is not technically a grain but it can be used to substitute for bulgur and rice in recipes.

Tahini: Sesame Seed Paste. Tahini is available in most grocery stores and for certain in Middle Eastern grocery stores

Orange Blossom Water: It is a flavoring ingredient. It is available in most grocery stores.

Recipe Index

A

B

C

G

H

K

L

M

N

O

P

R

S

T

Ingredient Index

A

B

C

D

E

Q

R

S

T